CONTENTS

WHO THIS KIT IS FOR

The StartUp Kit is for anyone considering or starting a business.

You may have been thinking about how you can make a living from a particular passion, hobby or skill. Perhaps you're working a day job and already making sales on the side – now you want to take it to the next level. Maybe you haven't hit upon the right idea yet; you just know in your heart that you want to be your own boss.

This kit offers all the tools, tips and templates you need to succeed. It'll help you find an idea, spot a gap in the market and start your own small business. Doing so will be one of the best moves you've ever made!

ABOUT THE AUTHOR

Emma Jones is a business expert, author and founder of small business network Enterprise Nation. Her books include *Working 5 to 9, Go Global: How to take your business to the world* and *Turn Your Talent Into a Business*.

Following a five-year career at an international accounting firm, Emma started her first business at 27. That business was sold 18 months later, and the experience led to Emma's next venture, Enterprise Nation.

Its website (**www.enterprisenation.com**) was launched in 2006 and became the most popular site for home business owners in the UK, attracting over 100,000 visitors each month.

In eight years, Enterprise Nation has grown into a community of over 75,000 homegrown businesses that find help and support on its website, in its books and at live events. The company has launched a membership scheme, which helps members promote their business, take their venture to the next level and have their views represented to government.

In 2011, Emma was a co-founder of StartUp Britain, a national campaign to encourage more people to start a business.

Emma was awarded an MBE for services to enterprise in July 2012.

“ There is a satisfaction in creating your own enterprise that is unknown to those who work for others. **”**

– Lord Young of Graffham

FOREWORD
BY LORD YOUNG OF GRAFFHAM

As a serial entrepreneur and an occasional politician I have seen how enterprise changes people's lives, including my own. I often boast that I haven't worked since March 1961, when I left my then-employer and set up my first business. Of course, working for yourself is not always fun – it can be hard, often lonely, not always successful – but at the end of the day there is a satisfaction in creating your own enterprise that is unknown to those who work for others.

And this is not just a selfish interest. Our economy today is made up of over five million small firms, of which over a million were created in the last two years. I believe that another million will be created over the next few years and yours could be one of them.

Some 30 years ago I created the very first business start-up programme. Some of the companies that started all those years ago are now amongst the biggest in the land; but the vast majority are still small firms that have provided a lifetime's income for their founders. More recently, I launched the StartUp Loan (**www.startuploans.co.uk**) programme that is designed to help anyone create a business plan and then get a loan, as well as benefit from mentor support.

I believe the opportunity to meet a mentor, to talk through a possible business plan, to appreciate what is required to start, will benefit nearly all who go through the process. The limits of your business will then be up to you.

This kit is your first step to your new life. Read it and take advantage of all it offers. From this moment onwards, a new door opens.

LORD YOUNG OF GRAFFHAM | @THELORDYOUNG

Lord Young is Enterprise Adviser to the Prime Minister

" In this kit, I'll show you how to start and grow a successful business in your spare time, from home and on a budget. "

LET'S GET STARTED

There has never been a better time to start a business and in 2013 record numbers of people did just that. According to the StartUp Britain Barometer, 520,400 people formed a limited company in the space of 12 months. A survey called the Global Entrepreneurship Monitor revealed the highest number of people starting a business since research began in 1999. This was followed by data from the Department for Business, Innovation and Skills, showing the number of small businesses having increased to 4.9 million – another record high.

Why is this happening? Simple: because it's now perfectly possible to start and grow a successful business

- in your spare time
- from home
- on a budget
- with help from friends and others.

In this kit, I'll show you how it's done.

People in their thousands are spotting gaps in the market or turning their hobbies into a successful venture. They are embracing free or low-cost technology to promote themselves and make sales, with a good number of these sales coming from overseas customers. Having access to the internet means you can start a business on a Monday and be trading with the world by Wednesday.

The start-up companies profiled in this book discuss how they got going and how they accessed the invaluable support that's helped them along the way. They are selling everything from hip flasks to shoes, luxury luggage, gourmet recipes and board games. Their products may be different, but the owners of these businesses all talk about the opportunities available to them and the joy of having the freedom to work how and where they like. They are of all ages. Many started in employment. A good number are already going global.

If you'd like to experience the same sense of independence and excitement, all you have to do is follow some basic steps: come up with an idea, do some research and marketing, offer good customer service – and you're in business!

In the following pages I'll walk you through everything that's involved in doing this successfully.

EMMA JONES | @EMMALJONES

**With thanks to StartUp Saturday
sponsors and supporters**

go.co

HOW TO ACCESS YOUR OFFERS

The StartUp Kit comes with a range of offers from top brands. These deals are on everything from domain registration to website builders and business cards. They are ideal for your new start-up.

To find out more about the offers available, and to take advantage of them, head to:

www.enterprisenation.com/offers

You don't have to access all the offers at once if you don't want to; you can come back at any time.

We'll be adding new offers throughout the year and you'll be able to access those too.

And that's not all ...

As well as accessing the partner offers, you can also use the above link to download templates, get hold of resources and stay bang up-to-date on the latest small business news!

I. PREPARE

With any undertaking, preparation is key.
Whether baking a cake, going on a date or
heading on holiday, time is given over to
research and preparation. Starting a business
is no different. Dedicate time to coming up
with an idea, ensuring it's viable, and
registering with the relevant bodies. These are
the base ingredients required for a successful
enterprise!

1. COMING UP WITH AN IDEA

Ingredient number one: a business idea! Many people tell me they would like to start a business but what's holding them back is not having an idea. It's easy to come up with one. Ask yourself these three questions:

1. Is there a gap in the market?

Have you tried to buy something that you just can't find? Could others be looking for the same thing? If so, this presents a market opportunity. It was a gap in the market that encouraged Esther Thompson of Tea Huggers to leave a big job at the BBC for a life of self-employment.

2. What is my passion/hobby/skill?

Many people are turning what they love into a way of making a living. Best of all, when you work on what you enjoy, doing it never really feels like work. Are you a dab hand at design? Have an eye for photography? A head for figures? These skills and hobbies can easily be turned into a business.

3. Is there something someone else is doing that I can do better myself?

If you've bought something and been unimpressed, why not step in, set up a business, and provide a better offer? Many good ideas stem from spotting products and services that can simply be improved upon or offered for less.

* * *

Your idea will develop over time. Don't be surprised if in 12 months' time it looks different to when you started out. This is okay. Business ideas tend to get refined over time; your offer will get sharper the more experience you gain in the marketplace. What's important is to get started with the beginnings of an idea – there'll be time to develop it as you get feedback from customers and input from others.

CASE STUDY

NAME: **Esther Thompson** | BUSINESS: **Tea Huggers**

Esther Thompson had been drinking herbal tea for 15 years and was becoming increasingly disillusioned with the products on the market.

"Often the tea smelt delicious but the taste didn't deliver. Over the years I noticed that other countries took tea-drinking much more seriously than the British, which didn't seem right to me. I became convinced there was a gap in the market for a high-quality herbal tea range that was packed full of flavour."

After this, Esther – formerly head of communications at the BBC's commercial unit – spent a year researching and planning.

"Fortunately I have a few friends who have launched very successful businesses so I used them as a sounding board. When my business plan was in decent shape I managed to speak to some experts in the industry who helped me refine my ideas and strengthen the proposition. I went through so many different versions of the business plan, but each time it became stronger and stronger."

The business, Tea Huggers, was officially launched in December 2013, when Esther hired a master tea-blender who helped design the tea range and source the ingredients.

"For the packaging I used a local website to track down a designer. Four people pitched for the work and luckily I found a highly experienced packaging designer with experience in the tea industry who lived in my neighbourhood. It's amazing the contacts you can find through your local online community!"

When it came to sales, Esther opted again to keep it local. She visited local food stores and supermarkets to talk them through her product and ideas.

"This helped me refine the product with advice from people who would ultimately be my customers, so when I had the finished product I had the confidence to walk into any shop, big or small, and pitch my products. I've been blown away by the positive reaction."

Online sales currently make up the bulk of company revenue, but Esther is working towards selling more of her tea range through stockists. She's also planning a stand at a trade fair to help generate leads with key stockists, whilst maintaining online promotion to attract new site visitors – and keep existing ones coming back.

"With all my online orders I've put in a little luggage label with a message asking people to take a picture of the tea they've bought with the luggage label. People have posted them on Facebook and it's really helped create a buzz around the brand."

As for what the future brings, Esther is keen to secure more routes to market and to look at elements of the business that can be outsourced so this hardworking mum of two can make the time she spends on Tea Huggers as efficient as possible.

After that, she'll most certainly be needing a nice cup of herbal tea!

● **www.teahuggers.co.uk** | @teahuggers

TOP TIP: "Write your idea down, talk to experts, refine and repeat."

50 ideas for businesses

These are all ideas and businesses we have seen and profiled on Enterprise Nation. Many of them started as '5 to 9' businesses. In other words, a business started whilst the entrepreneur was in full-time study or employment. More on that later!

Blogger
Vlogger
Social media advisor
eBay trader
Online store owner
Giftware maker
Giftware seller
Artisan
Cupcake maker
Cosmetics producer
Hair and make-up artist
Origami artist
Picture artist
Furniture marker
Jewellery designer
Footwear designer
Fashion designer

Clothing producer
Toymaker
Party organiser
DJ
Musician
Magician
Beer producer
Events organiser
Wedding planner
Mystery shopper
Image consultant
Fitness advisor
Personal trainer
Photographer
Accountant
Lawyer

Translator
IT services
App developer
Software developer
Print and web designer
Network marketer
Pet care
Product manufacturer
E-learning provider
Facebook developer
Magazine publisher
T-shirt maker
Papercrafter
Dance instructor
Perfumer
Balloon decorator
Street advertiser

There are so many possibilities. You might even have too many ideas. In which case, don't be afraid to spend some time on all of them and, wherever possible, let the customer decide – try them out in small ways and see what gets the warmest response.

Niche is nice

When coming up with your idea, bear in mind that niche businesses are often ideal. Meeting the needs of a very well-defined audience helps keep your efforts focused and your offering clear in a crowded market. It also means success should naturally consolidate itself. So rather than just selling clothes, why not become the go-to place for men's blazers, and instead of offering food to suit all palates, how about re-inventing pizza so it offers a balanced meal to consumers interested in healthy eating?

With a niche business:

- **you keep marketing costs low**, as your audience is well-defined; you know where your audience are and understand the kind of marketing messages to which they will respond
- **customer loyalty remains high**, as you become the expert in your field or the only provider of certain products; customers will want to stay with you and benefit from the specialist product or service you offer.

FRIENDS AND FAMILY FOCUS GROUP: Talk to family and friends and ask them where they think your talents lie. They might just help you discover your business idea in an area you hadn't thought of.

The niche list

Here are some businesses I've come across that have benefited from having a clear niche. A few of them are profiled in this guide:

- Tilly & The Buttons (**www.tillyandthebuttons.com**) | *Dress-making tips and tutorials for women who want to take control of their style*
- Guilt Free Gourmet (**www.jordanbourke.com**) | *Healthy food for all ocassions*
- Collie Wobbles (**www.colliewobbles.co.uk**) | *Border Collie/sheepdog-related products*

- Rock 'n' Roll Bride (www.rocknrollbride.com) | *For brides wanting a rock 'n' roll wedding*
- Cambridge Raincoat Company (www.cambridgeraincoats.co.uk) | *Fashion raincoats for people who ride upright bicycles*
- Stow London (www.stowlondon.co.uk) | *Irresistible luxury for stylish travel*

* * *

Whatever the idea, good ones tend be based on what you enjoy, what people will buy and something that improves on what's already available. Think about how you can fashion your idea so it has a clear purpose for a clearly defined audience.

Use this template to help come up with your idea:

Template 1: What's the Big Idea?

Have I spotted a gap in the market?

What is my passion/hobby/skill?

Is there something I've seen that I can do better myself?

What about buying into someone else's idea via a franchise?

An idea as part of the package

If you're not able to settle on a viable idea of your own, consider buying into someone else's idea. You can do so through a franchise or signing up as a party-plan consultant and/or direct sales agent. Benefit from being your own boss whilst having the support of a central team and the proven idea that comes with it!

Here are a few top franchise or party-plan opportunities:

- My Secret Kitchen | www.mysecretkitchen.co.uk
- Jamie at Home | www.jamieathome.com
- The Pampered Chef | www.pamperedchef.co.uk
- Girlie Gardening | www.girliegardening.com
- Avon | www.avon.uk.com
- Kleeneze | www.kleeneze.com
- Neal's Yard | www.nealsyardremedies.com
- Maid2Clean | www.maid2clean.co.uk
- Razzamataz | www.razzamataz.co.uk

- Travel Counsellors | www.travelcounsellors.co.uk
- Tatty Bumpkin | www.tattybumpkin.com
- Barrett & Coe | www.barrettandcoe.co.uk
- Barking Mad | www.barkingmad.uk.com
- Curves | www.curves.co.uk
- Raring2Go! | www.raring2go.co.uk
- PyjamaDrama | www.pyjamadrama.com
- Usborne Books | www.usborne.com
- Captain Tortue Group | www.captaintortuegroup.com

USEFUL LINKS
- Direct Selling Association | www.dsa.org.uk
- British Franchise Association | www.thebfa.org

" Choose a business idea that you are passionate about. You're going to be spending a lot of time on it. And when you're working on something you love, it stops being work and feels more like fun. **"**

– Michael Acton-Smith,
founder, Moshi Monsters

2. RESEARCH THE MARKET

Y ou have your idea. Turning it into a business requires some research, followed by a straightforward exercise in building that research into a plan. Here's how to go about it.

First, **research your potential customers**, the competition and a price point by visiting competitors' sites, online trade sites/forums, reading reports, and seeking intelligence from experts.

Look for data and comments that will answer the following questions:

- What is the number of potential customers you can serve, and how do these customers like to be served?

- What are their core characteristics and spending patterns, and who are their key influencers?

- Who is currently serving your market?

- Where are your potential customers going for their goods and services?

- What do they like about what they're getting and, more importantly, what do they dislike (as this opens up opportunities for you to improve on the status quo)?

In view of the above, what price can you charge for your product/service?

Price yourself at a rate that's competitive with other providers in the market, that takes into account the amount of time, personal service and added value you offer, and that will turn a profit at the end of the day.

WHAT AM I WORTH? How much do you think customers or clients would pay for your product or service? Take a look at how similar offerings are priced and talk to people about how much they'd be willing to pay. Then talk to suppliers to check you can source materials and deliver at a price that covers your costs. Since starting a business from home (which I recommend you do!) will save you lots of money, you can pass some of these savings onto your customers. It will give you an edge over other businesses. But don't undercharge for the expertise and knowledge you offer. Only consider charging less for work that will reflect well on your business and boost your reputation, perhaps in the media or with a particularly important customer.

You can also source primary, or firsthand, data by conducting a survey or posing questions on social media channels.

Survey tools

- SurveyMonkey | www.surveymonkey.com
- Wufoo | www.wufoo.com

Social media channels

- Twitter | www.twitter.com
- Facebook | www.facebook.com
- LinkedIn | www.linkedin.com

Or, of course, you can hit the streets with a clipboard!

The subject of our next case study – Philip Crilly of Eatibbles – went online and to the British Library IP Centre for the research he needed for his new business. Start working on your own market research plan by completing Template 2 later in this chapter.

The name game

Coming up with an idea and carrying out research will get you thinking about what to name your business. If selling your knowledge, the company could be named after you – for example, 'Emma Jones Advisory Services'. In which case, job done! But if you're looking for something else, think of a name that:

- is easy to spell
- has an available domain name
- is not already registered with Companies House (use the free web-check service to access existing company names at www.companieshouse.gov.uk)
- people will remember.

You might want to protect the name with a trademark. See later for information on how to go about that.

If you get stuck, visit Enterprise Nation (www.enterprisenation.com) where you will find people who can help you: the site is buzzing with talented copywriters and wordsmiths.

CASE STUDY

NAME: **Philip Crilly** | BUSINESS: **Eatibbles**

In his day job as a pharmacist, Philip Crilly comes into contact with customers with many different healthcare needs. It was this day-to-day experience that gave Philip the idea for his business, Eatibbles, the gluten-free food brand.

"I didn't feel the products on offer for coeliac patients and those with gluten intolerances were of a high enough standard. I decided to attend a course at Leiths Cookery School (www.leiths.com) and then experiment with different gluten-free ingredients to try and come up with better quality alternatives. The first product I perfected was gluten-free granola and this is now available in three flavours. Indeed, it's now my business!"

Philip did a lot of online research ahead of starting the business; looking to other countries like America, Australia and South Africa, to see what similar businesses were doing.

"I used the Business IP Centre at the British Library, which is a huge resource. Every marketing report you could ever need is there and I was able to research how big the gluten-free market is and what trends are becoming more popular. I also connected with other people working in the gluten-free market to get their opinions on my product and to ask their advice on how to grow the business."

One of the tips Philip picked up from his research was that when making a food product from home you need to inform your local authority.

"It's a very simple process and all the information you need can be found at the local authority website. I also completed a food safety course online and a course about making gluten-free products to make sure I was working according to the correct recommendations.

"In addition to researching online around the business concept, I did a lot of research into packaging and found a supplier who specialises in making packaging products for cereals. I sought advice from a food marketing company and emailed businesses whose packaging I admire to see if they could advise me on the best suppliers."

Following on from making sales to friends and family, Philip is now selling at local food markets and online.

"It's so rewarding watching people sample my products at the market, love them, and then buy them. Making the product myself makes it personal, so every sale feels like an achievement."

There have been marketing successes, including a meeting with Greg Wallace of *MasterChef* fame and hosting the Eatibbles launch at Greg's restaurant, as well as winning the Shell LiveWIRE Grand Ideas Award.

"This was a massive boost. Not only did we win £1,000 in prize money for the business, we also received lots of great publicity which really highlighted the brand to lots more people and boosted sales. We've been featured in the *Guardian*, in HSBC Business marketing literature, and I picked up lots of new contacts from writing a 12-week start-up challenge on the Enterprise Nation blog."

Going forward, Philip wants to find a manufacturing partner to help scale the business.

"Making everything from home has its limitations so having someone else manufacture the granola will allow me to expand the marketing and sales for the business. I'm also working on new products and looking into new niche markets."

What's impressive is that Philip has come so far whilst holding on to the day job. In fact, the entrepreneurial skills he's picked up on account of the business have even lead to a promotion!

"Since launching the business I've always been very open with my employer and they have been very supportive. When an opportunity came up recently for a promotion I was given the job as a direct result of my business venture. Starting your own business allows you to demonstrate so many different skills and this has had a positive impact on my career. Juggling a career with a new business can have its challenges but with some careful organisation you can get the balance right."

- **www.eatibbles.co.uk** | @eatibbles

TOP TIP: "Don't be afraid to make mistakes. Learn from them fast and keep moving on."

Template 2: Market Research

How big is the market?

What is the number of potential customers I can serve and how do these customers like to be served?

What are their characteristics, spending patterns and who are their key influences?

Who is currently serving my market?

Where are my potential customers going for their goods and services?

What do they like about what they're getting, and, more importantly, what do they dislike?

What price can I charge for my product/service?

What's competitive and takes into account the amount of time, personal service and added value that I offer?

SWOT analysis

With your idea, and now your research in-hand that supports it, prepare a SWOT analysis. This stands for: **S**trengths, **W**eaknesses, **O**pportunities, **T**hreats and looks as follows:

Strengths

What are my strengths?

What can I do better than anyone else?

What resources do I have?

What's my unique selling point?

Weaknesses

What are my weaknesses?

What should I avoid?

Where do I lack skills?

What might hinder my success?

Opportunities

What opportunities do I see?

Does my idea tap into any trends?

Are there any emerging technologies that could help my idea?

Has there been anything in the news related to my idea?

Threats

What threats might I face?

Who's my competition?

Does changing technology affect my idea?

Template 3: SWOT Analysis

Strengths

What are my strengths?

Weaknesses

What are my weaknesses?

Opportunities

What opportunities do I see?

Threats

What threats might I face?

3. WRITE A PLAN

A business plan will act as your map. It will guide the business from start to growth, with reference to milestones along the way.

The plan will include information about how you intend to get started and what your ultimate objectives are – and how you aim to get from one to the other. You might want to start a business and sell it in a few years' time, or grow to a point where you wouldn't want to grow anymore.

Of course, you'll need to refer to resources: what you have already, what you'll need and how you'll pay for it.

So, after coming up with an idea and doing your research, writing the business plan is your first practical step to starting your business. With it under your belt you can say, "I'm off!"

Or IMOFF. It's an easy way to remember the headings to include in your business plan: **I**dea, **M**arket, **O**perations, **F**inancials and **F**riends. Have these as headings in your plan and you've taken a big step closer to becoming your own boss.

Idea

What's your idea?

Market

Who will be your customers or clients? And who is your competition?

Operations

How will you develop the idea, promote it and provide good customer service?

Financials

Can you earn more than you spend, so that the business makes a profit? Do you need any funds to get started?

Friends

Do you have a support network on hand for when you need business advice? Are there complementary businesses you've identified with whom partnerships are a possibility?

Return regularly to your plan to check progress against targets or to make amends as you respond to new opportunities.

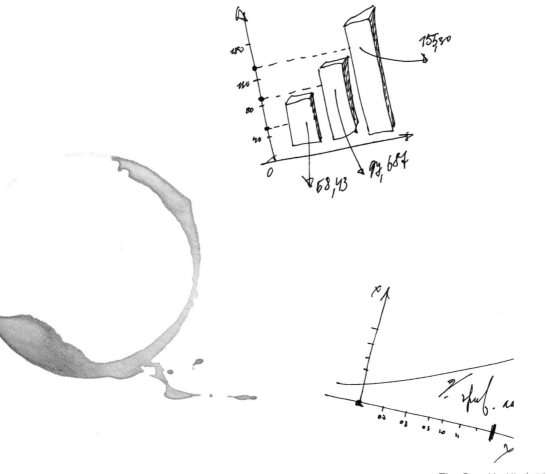

Business Plan
20xx–20xx
(This business plan is for a two-year cycle. You may choose to do a 12-month plan, two years or up to five years.)

Contents

Executive Summary

Summarise what's in the rest of the plan. Something like this:

The vision for ABC is to become the leading company for selling *abc* to *xyz*. This plan sets out how the vision will be achieved in the period 20xx–20xx. It outlines the product on offer, provides data on the market and shows how the company will be operating profitably within the first three months.

Having identified a clear gap in the market, I'm excited about the opportunity to start and build a successful business that will offer a quality product [or service] to a well-defined market.

A. Person
Founder, Company ABC

The Idea

Include here your 'elevator pitch'; what is your product and how will it benefit the customer?

This is the opportunity to explain the idea of the business in a few sentences.

* This title would be more like 'Advisory Board' if preparing the plan for a bank or funder.

The Market

Customers

Who will be your customers? Include the quantity, their demographic profile, geographic locations, social backgrounds; essentially any strong data that shows you know your audience.

Competition

Who is selling a similar product/service? How do you differ from them? What is your unique selling point?

You can do this by producing a table that lists the competition. Outline what makes you stand out in the market: is it that your service will be online, that you'll charge a different price, have an innovative marketing approach or offer the service with a special extra twist?

Operations

The CEO

You have come up with the idea for the business and you've done your research on the market. Now it's time for the reader to know a bit about you! Note your background, skills, experience and any credentials for running this business. Plus information on other key members of staff (if there are any).

Sourcing

If this applies to your business, refer to how you'll source your product/service. You may be making it yourself!

Sales & Marketing

How will you promote what you offer to your customers? Include a brief sales and marketing plan with headings like this:

Press – how many press releases do you plan to distribute each year and to which press channels: newspapers, magazines, radio, etc.?

Online – will you have your own blog/website? Mention other sites that you'll approach for reciprocal links.

Partners – what about marketing tie-ups with other companies selling to the same audience?

You know where your customers are, so let your marketing plan show that you'll reach them in print, online and even in the streets!

Systems

You've sourced the service/product and told customers about it. Refer here to the process customers will go through to buy from you and the systems you'll have in place to deliver in time and on budget. Systems that may include online ordering and payment, a professional call-handling service to take orders or maybe some specific software.

Financials

Last but not least come the figures. Make this as clear as possible and it's probably best to do it in table form:

	Year 1	Year 2
Revenue		
Overheads		
Office rent		
Salary		
Stock		
Technology		
Marketing		
Travel & expenses		
Projected profit		

Drawing up a simple financial forecast will highlight any need to borrow money.

Friends & Family

In starting and growing your business, will you call on friends and family for advice? If so, refer to this here; mention your board of advisors, your experts-on-call, your support network!

(See Chapter 16 for details on how to access expert advisors and find a mentor whose details you can also include here.)

Template 4: Business Plan

Use this template to write your own business plan.

Executive Summary

The Idea

The Market
Customers

Competition

Operations
The CEO

Sourcing

Sales & Marketing
Press

Online

Partners

Systems

Friends & Family

Financials

4. REGISTER THE COMPANY

When you set up in business, there are a couple of organisations you need to contact: Companies House and HM Revenue & Customs (HMRC). Before registering with either, have a think about the company status that suits you best.

Self-employed

This status means you are working for yourself. You keep records and accounts of your own activities and, in acting alone, get to keep all the profits – but are also solely liable for any debts.

Limited company

Limited companies exist in their own right, with the company's finances kept separate from the personal finances of its owners, so your liability is limited.

Partnership

If you'd like to be self-employed but want to work with a friend or colleague, consider a partnership. It means that two or more people share the risks, costs and workload.

Many of the companies featured in the following pages have formed a partnership. They all comment on how a mix of skills and experience is helping the business to grow.

IF YOU'RE UNSURE, ASK: The status of your company will affect how much admin you have to do and the kind of financial records that you need to keep and file. Take advice from your accountant or local tax office on which one to choose. See later for details on how to access free consultations with qualified accountants.

The business partner of Crafty Fox Market's Sinead Koehler, our next case study, also happens to be her husband!

CASE STUDY

NAME: **Sinead Koehler** | BUSINESS: **Crafty Fox Market**

In 2010 Sinead Koehler was traveling across town to sell her handmade jewellery at a market in North London and wondered why there weren't any opportunities to trade closer to home in South London.

"I decided the only thing to do was to put on my own event. I roped in my husband, Stephan, who had spent years promoting club nights in Dublin. We were very lucky that our friend Jimbobart was excited about the project too and was keen to be involved from the start. He came up with the visual identity of the fox character. Our first Christmas Market was in 2010. Shoppers loved the warm Crafty Fox atmosphere and were impressed by the range of work on offer. Many asked when the next event would be, so we decided to run with it."

The couple have since run a total of 11 Crafty Fox Markets, hosting 40–50 traders each time.

"We always strive to showcase as many new traders as possible as there are so many talented makers and artists out there. The volume of applications has been steadily increasing and we now receive around four applications for every available space. Selecting traders has become increasingly challenging, so in 2012 we began inviting expert guest curators to lend their expertise. This has an added advantage of keeping the markets fresh as each guest curator's personal taste is reflected in the final stall selections."

An opt-in mailing list has been a valuable tool enabling Sinead to directly communicate with people who have expressed interest in the company.

"The list grows on a daily basis. We have a sign-up form on our website and gather sign-ups at events."

As well as the markets, a new series of Crafty Fox Talks has been introduced to bring together the crafty community to listen to inspiring speakers and make connections.

"To date, each of the events has sold-out. This has helped to raise both revenue and profile for Crafty Fox and we're planning to expand both the markets and talks to new areas of London in the next year. Sourcing talented new traders and supporting those who are starting out with market trading will continue to be a key focus."

When it comes to how this couple manage to work and live together, Sinead explains that it took a while to clearly define respective roles.

"Over time our strengths and weaknesses came to the surface and fortunately we have complementary skill-sets. Stephan has a full-time job working in marketing so his time for Crafty Fox is more limited. I handle the day-to-day management of the business and all the admin that goes with it. When it comes to promoting each event, I'll typically manage everything online while Stephan will take the lead on offline activity like postering and flyering. Stephan acts as my sounding board for new ideas and helps with strategic thinking.

"For the first three years, we were both in full-time employment and ran Crafty Fox Market at evenings and weekends. For the past four months, I've been working two days a week on the business while looking after our young son the rest of the time. Stephan still has a full-time job so makes use of time outside working hours."

The couple are powering ahead with new opportunities for growth and Sinead continues to build profile by speaking at events – as well as hosting her own. With this kind of upbringing, you can only wonder if Koehler Junior will grow up to be a top notch entrepreneur himself.

- **www.craftyfoxmarket.co.uk** | @craftyfoxmarket

TOP TIP: "Just get started! I often meet people who have great ideas but never get around to putting them into practice. Getting started is often the hardest part."

See later for details on how to form a partnership agreement.

Being social

Should you decide to start a social enterprise – a business trading for social and environmental purposes – there are additional legal structures to consider, including:

- community interest company (CIC)
- industrial and provident society
- charitable status.

To find out more about launching a social enterprise or creating a CIC visit:

- Social Enterprise UK | **www.socialenterprise.org.uk**
- CIC Regulator | **www.cicregulator.gov.uk**
- 'Setting up a social enterprise' via GOV.UK | **www.gov.uk/set-up-a-social-enterprise**

Companies House

When registering with Companies House, there are three options from which to choose. You can buy a ready-made company from a company formation agent, incorporate a company yourself by sending documents and a registration fee to Companies House or register online via GOV.UK. If you decide to complete registration yourself, see form IN01 – application to register a company. It can be easier to go with a formation agent as they do the work on your behalf.

- **GOV.UK** | Incorporate via GOV.UK (**www.gov.uk/register-a-company-online**) and pay £15.

- **Self-incorporation** | Visit the new company registration page of the Companies House website: **bit.ly/dw1xcJ**. Complete form IN01. Post to Companies House with relevant fee. Standard service fee of £40 (documents processed in eight to ten days). Same-day service fee is £100.

- **Company formation agent** | Register with a formation agent such as Companies Made Simple (**www.companiesmadesimple.com**). Prices start at £16.99 for standard company registration.

HM Revenue & Customs

The rules on registering a new business with HM Revenue & Customs are pretty clear-cut. You are required to register as soon as you start earning from any business activity. As stated, you can choose to register as self-employed, as a partnership, or as a limited company. Each category has its own filing requirements, as we'll explore now.

Sole trader/self-employed

The calculation of tax and National Insurance owing is done through self-assessment. You either need to complete a form CWF1, or simply call the newly self-employed business helpline. It should be done by 5 October after the end of the tax year in which you started your business to avoid a fine.

- Form CWF1 | **www.hmrc.gov.uk/forms/cwf1.pdf**

- Helpline for the newly self-employed | 0845 915 4515

It's not onerous to complete the form and, once registered, you'll be classified as self-employed and sent a self-assessment tax return each year, which you complete, showing your income and expenses from self-employment as well as details of your employment elsewhere (if that applies).

You will be subject to tax and National Insurance on any profits you make, but the good news is that any losses incurred can be offset against your employed income (if you have any), which could even result in a tax rebate.

Depending on your turnover and how straightforward your tax affairs are, you may be able to simply fill out the short tax return (SA103s). However, this cannot be self-selected, nor is it on the HMRC website or orderable; HMRC will send it to you automatically if they think you qualify, based on information given in the previous year's return. If you have turnover below £77,000 (at the time of writing), it's likely that you will qualify. As ever, though, it will depend on individual circumstances, and the law (and various criteria it uses) may change!

Deadlines

Self-assessment tax return deadlines are as follows:

- paper tax returns should be received by HMRC by 31 October
- online tax returns should be completed by 31 January (giving you an extra three months).

Useful links

- Leaflet SE1 – 'Thinking of working for yourself?' | www.hmrc.gov.uk/leaflets/se1.pdf
- Helping you understand self assessment and your tax return, HMRC | www.hmrc.gov.uk/sa

Partnership

According to HMRC, a partnership is where:

"Two or more people set up a business. Each partner is personally responsible for all the business debts, even if the debt was caused by another partner. As partners, each pays income tax on their share of the business profits through self-assessment, as well as National Insurance."

In terms of filing requirements, each partner should complete a partnership supplementary page as part of their individual self-assessment tax return. This is in addition to a partnership return, which has to be submitted by one nominated partner and show each partner's share of profits/losses.

Deadlines

The deadlines for partnership tax returns are as follows:

- paper tax returns should be received by HMRC by 31 October
- online tax returns should be completed by 31 January (giving you an extra three months).

Limited company

Limited companies exist in their own right, with the company's finances distinct from the personal finances of the owners. What this means is that the company is liable for any debts, not the individual owners, as is the case if you are self-employed or in a partnership.

In April 2008 it became legal to form and run a limited company with just one person, without the need to involve anyone else (prior to this you also needed a company secretary). As noted, you can form a new limited company by registering with Companies House via GOV.UK (**www.gov.uk/limited-company-formation**) or by using a company creation agent.

As well as registering with Companies House, you also need to let HMRC know you are operating as a limited company. And you will need to set up and register a PAYE scheme, as you are an employee of the company.

- Register PAYE scheme | **www.hmrc.gov.uk/newemployers**
- New employer's helpline | 0845 60 70 143

In terms of filing requirements, you should complete a self-assessment company tax return at the end of the accounting period. The return will show the company's taxable profits and whether any corporation tax is owed, and can be filed online at www.hmrc.gov.uk/ct.

The return should also be filed with Companies House to comply with the Companies Act 2006. This can be done free of charge, using the online WebFiling service at Companies House: ewf.companieshouse.gov.uk

On your returns, you can claim an element of your expenses for working from home. You can also claim travelling expenses, subsistence and a proportion of your phone calls.

Deadlines

Whereas filing deadlines for self-assessment and partnership tax returns are specific dates, that is not the case with company tax returns, which must be filed 12 months after the end of your company's corporation tax accounting period.

IN GOOD ORDER: Keep records of your business dealings – this will make it much easier to complete tax returns when the time comes. Keep hold of **receipts** of business-related **purchases**; **copies of invoices** to customers; **bank statements**, especially if you don't yet have a separate account for the business (it is worth starting one); **utility bills** (if you are starting the business from home and using part of the house for business), which can be claimed as a business expense and so reduce your tax bill.

For advice from HMRC on good record keeping, visit:
www.hmrc.gov.uk/startingup/keeprecs.htm

VAT

Whichever company status you choose, if your business turns over more than £79,000 (in the 2013/14 tax year), or you think your turnover will soon exceed this amount, you should also register for value added tax (VAT).

You can voluntarily register at any time. Being VAT-registered can bring credibility with certain customers, but adding VAT to your invoices may make you more expensive than competitors and you will have to file a VAT return four times a year.

- 'How and when to register for VAT', HMRC |
  www.hmrc.gov.uk/vat/start/register

Accountant accompaniment

Talk to a qualified accountant about the structure that is best for your business. And consider employing their services to complete your tax returns. Even if your accounts are very simple, it is well worth seeking professional advice, particularly as the rules and regulations can change frequently and without warning.

You can access up to three free consultations with an accountant through the Institute of Chartered Accountants of England & Wales (ICAEW)'s Business Advice Service: **www.businessadviceservice.com**

Useful links

- 'Starting a Business', HMRC | **www.hmrc.gov.uk/startingup**
- 'Tax Help – and advice for small business' | **www.businesslink.gov.uk/taxhelp**

5. PROTECT THE BRAND

You have now registered with Companies House and HM Revenue & Customs. Your final consideration should be your intellectual property. You may decide to register a trademark to protect your company name or brand or, if you've come up with a unique invention, a patent. Registering either means that companies can't come along and use your name or invention without your permission.

The four forms of IP

There are four different kinds of intellectual property that you can protect:

1. Patents: These protect what makes things work. For example, says the Intellectual Property Office (IPO), "what makes a wheel turn or the chemical formula of your favourite fizzy drink".

2. Trademarks: These are "signs (like words and logos) that distinguish goods and services in the marketplace".

3. Designs: What a logo or product looks like: "from the shape of an aeroplane to a fashion item".

4. Copyright: An automatic right that comes into existence for anything written or recorded.

Register and protect your intellectual property by visiting the UK Intellectual Property Office website (www.ipo.gov.uk). Charlie Ashworth is founder of Venture Proof (www.ventureproof.com) a company that helps small businesses protect their IP. Charlie says:

"It doesn't matter what product your business makes, or what service it provides, every enterprise is regularly generating and applying a considerable amount of intellectual property. This is a prized and valued possession – and one you should aim to protect to secure your venture."

6. TAKE CARE OF HOUSEHOLD ADMIN

When starting out, you'll likely be starting from home – your own, your parents' or maybe a friend's. It's the best way to start, keeping costs low and the commute short. In other words: more time and money for the business.

You'll probably be outsourcing work as opposed to employing staff, so there's no need for lots of people to come into the office each day. And you can meet clients and contacts in the local hotel or serviced work space. It's also good to know you're not alone in starting at home – over 70% of businesses do. You may have a few questions around household admin and who you need to tell. Here are the answers.

Q: Do I need planning permission?

A: You'll only need planning permission to base the business at home if you answer 'yes' to any of these questions:

- will your home no longer be used mainly as a private residence?
- will your business result in a marked rise in traffic or people calling?
- will your business involve any activities that are unusual in a residential area?
- will your business disturb the neighbours at unreasonable hours or create other forms of nuisance such as noise or smells?

If your house is pretty much going to remain a house, with your business quietly accommodated within it, then permission won't be required. If you're unsure, contact your local council to seek their views (**www.planningportal.gov.uk**).

Q: Do I need to tell the local authority I'm working from home?

A: Depends on whether you pass the planning test. If you need planning permission, you'll have to inform your local authority. If you don't, then the only benefit of telling them is that they'll charge you business rates (rather than council tax) on the part of the house being used for business purposes – not really much of an incentive! Business rates are different in each area and something that should be agreed with your local authority.

Q: Do I need to tell the landlord?

A: Yes, it's best to let them know that you will be working from home. Good news is, it was announced by the government on 1 November 2010 that social landlords should review any contracts prohibiting people from working from home, making it much easier for people in social housing to use living space as work space. Since then we've seen some social landlords such as London & Quadrant (www.lqgroup.org.uk) organise business training for tenants. A welcome sight.

Q: What about my insurance provider? Do they need to know?

A: Yes, do inform your insurance company. Tell them about the equipment and stock you have at home. An upgrade from domestic to a business policy is not expensive so don't be put off in making this call. Your insurance provider is likely to recommend that you also take out public liability insurance in case anyone who comes to visit suffers an injury in or around your home office. See the next page for a guide to all kinds of insurance.

Q: Do I need protection for when customers and contacts come to visit?

A: Yes, carry out a health and safety check, which is easy to do by following the steps set out by the Health and Safety Executive (www.hse.gov.uk) in their *Homeworking* guide (available at bit.ly/aGDc8N).

Q: Should I tell the neighbours?

A: Yes. When working from home, it's worth keeping your neighbours firmly on side. You don't want them getting annoyed by any deliveries or distractions. If you know of a time when there'll be an unusual amount of activity in your home office, let them know in advance and perhaps send a bottle of wine or gift to compensate.

INSURANCE INS-AND-OUTS

There are different categories of insurance which you need to know about to secure the policy that's right for you. The main ones are:

1. **PROFESSIONAL INDEMNITY** – relevant to businesses offering services and knowledge. Provides protection if you receive a claim alleging a negligent act, error or omission committed by you in the course of the conduct of your professional business.

2. **PUBLIC LIABILITY** – advisable to have if clients are visiting your home office and/or you are supplying goods to consumers. This will protect you in the event of potential injury to business visitors and/or damages arising from the supply or sale of goods which have caused injury to a third party or their property.

3. **BUSINESS INTERRUPTION** – covers your potential loss of revenue following a material damage loss.

4. **EMPLOYER'S LIABILITY** – only applies when you have employees. Offers protection in the event of death or injury to them sustained in the course of their employment.

5. **MOTOR INSURANCE** – this is different to standard car insurance, which does not include business use. If you have a vehicle dedicated for business, you should buy motor insurance or get a business extension on your car insurance policy when using your existing car for business travel.

6. **HOME INSURANCE** – you are likely to already have a home insurance policy but this will generally not cover business activities carried out at home or business equipment within the home. Speak to your insurance provider and upgrade to a business policy. This is not usually costly but it will ensure you're protected.

Creating the perfect work environment

Wherever you've chosen to set up shop, create the perfect work environment by following this quick checklist to ensure you're working profitably and productively.

Find dedicated space

Try to create an area at home that functions as your dedicated workspace. That way you can better adjust into business mode. It's also useful for making clear to friends and family that when you're in your home office, you're working.

This dedicated space could be a spare room, in the attic, under the stairs, or even the garden shed.

Invest in a good desk and chair

You could be spending a good few hours each day at the desk and in your chair, so be sure they're both sturdy and comfortable. Buy a chair that's designed for computer use – and try it out first. The back experts say your feet should be flat on the floor and your back straight.

When it comes to computers, the top of your monitor or laptop screen should be at eye level and about an arm's length away from you. There are all sorts of docks that can help with this, but there's also no harm in using a sturdy pile of books and an external mouse/keyboard to achieve the same end.

Have a vision

Put a vision board up on the wall and stick pictures on it that represent your personal and business ambitions: places you want to visit, targets for the company, and people you enjoy spending time with. Glance at it each day. Remind yourself of everything you're working for.

A SPRING CLEAN: Wondering what to do with all the stuff in the room that you want to use as your home office? Rent storage with a company like Bizspace (www.biz space.co.uk), Access Self Storage (www.accessstorage.com) or Big Yellow (www.bigyellow.co.uk) and have your goods accessible but out of the way, or give them to a recycling company so that your unwanted items can go to a home that does want them!

Roam free

Install Wi-Fi so it's possible to work from anywhere on the property. To get started you need a wireless router. You may have received one free from your internet service provider. If not, check out respectable suppliers such as Netgear (www.netgear.co.uk). See 'Getting connected' in the next chapter if you need support.

PETS AND PLANTS: Having plants in your home office can reduce work-stress, experts say. Seeing a growth in greenery can also help you feel less alone, and it helps with humidity levels, dust and productivity. Likewise, pets are known to reduce stress and can be an excellent source of company!

Support on tap

And finally, surround yourself with supporters. Friends or family, peers in online forums, contacts met at events; they can all help when it comes to celebrating your success or raising your spirits on a day that doesn't quite go as planned.

Eleanor Stuart, profiled in Chapter 11, found a wealth of support in her own industry sector from people who were also illustrators:

"At the outset I turned to other illustrators and designers whose work I really loved. I found so many helpful people who were only too happy to share their wisdom and support a fellow illustrator up the ladder."

Charlotte Faull has benefited from the support of her business partner/husband, as well as the start-up community, both online and off . . .

CASE STUDY

NAME: **Charlotte Faull** | BUSINESS: **Chartwell and G**

It was the willing words of her husband that encouraged Charlotte Faull to get started with her own business. Since then, she hasn't looked back.

"I was working long hours in a windowless office in the City. With the encouragement of my husband, along with a shared desire to change our lifestyle, I quit to start Chartwell and G. Initially our plan was to focus on printed, British-made pure silk cover-ups, but through the roller coaster of the start-up process, our ideas and plan changed into the product range we now have: hand-made, high-end British clothing and accessories with a minimalist and refined aesthetic."

At the beginning, Charlotte went online and to events for start-up advice and support.

"The internet is an incredible resource – Enterprise Nation and the government's www.gov.uk/business were particularly helpful, along with UK Trade & Investment and Enterprise Nation events. In fact, I think networking has been our most effective marketing tool so far. I don't particularly enjoy it but it has been invaluable. There is a real sense of community among start-ups and entrepreneurs and I've been delighted to be so warmly welcomed into it!"

Starting the business has moved Charlotte a step closer to the lifestyle she was after, one that involves working with her husband, Gareth.

"Working with my husband has been surprisingly fantastic. He works full-time from home and funds our business. We work and live together 24/7! We have different strengths; Gareth is particularly good with detail and IT, and I'm stronger on the strategy/marketing side. Combined, this really works. We both design and I think the great thing is that we don't have egos. We started this business to change our lifestyle so its success is mutually beneficial."

This entrepreneurial couple, who originally hail from New Zealand, were keen to keep production in Britain but found this particular aspect of the business a challenge.

"Finding the right suppliers and manufacturers has been frustrating but we were determined to find a solution. We have found a team of talented London-based freelance seamstresses which has enabled us to grow: keeping costs low yet still producing high quality hand-made products."

Charlotte is getting products to market through a stockist in Chelsea who approached the company just a couple of weeks after they launched their online estore.

"As well as selling online and through stockists in the UK, we are exploring international markets where we think there will be high demand for the products. Having handmade products limits the growth of the business to some extent, as we're very reliant on our freelance seamstresses, but we're aiming to be stocked in our key target markets and develop the brand internationally.'

That's one bright view. From a windowless office to a world of opportunity; it's what being in business for yourself is all about.

● **www.chartwellandg.co.uk** | @chartwellandg

TOP TIP: "Invest early on in trade-marking your brand, and ensure you decide on a name that is not only unique in the UK, but globally. Secure domain and social media names before submitting your trademark application."

Leaving home

For those days when you'd rather work outside the four walls of the home office, or if an external office is right for you from the start, find available space in enterprise hubs, co-working spaces, government buildings and serviced offices. All needs and budgets catered for! Neardesk (**www.neardesk.com**) is a new start-up that enables you to search for desk or office space within your budget and within a radius of where you want to work.

7. YOUR TECH SETUP

P utting together a tech setup for your new business needn't mean starting from scratch or spending lots of money. Once your business starts to grow, you can upgrade your tech as and when money becomes available.

To start with, there are affordable and free solutions that can get you up and running in no time at all. Chances are, you have some of them already.

So, let's take a look at what you might already have and what you might need to buy. We'll separate them by hardware and software.

Hardware

Computer

When starting out, using a shared computer will be just fine. Bear in mind, however, that in the first few months of starting your business, you may find yourself working more hours than usual trying to put it all together. So let your friends and family know you may be hogging the computer!

Also, when your business starts to grow, the information you collect – info on your customers, clients and contacts; including financial details – will become more and more valuable. You might then start to think twice about sharing your computer with other people.

You may already have your own laptop. If you don't, when you've got a bit of money behind you, look into buying one for your new business. Budget laptops start at around £300, but when buying a computer it sometimes pays to buy the best you can afford in order to prepare for the future. Look out for these key features:

Processor

The processor is the speed of your computer. The higher the number, the faster your computer can run.

Memory

More memory (RAM) improves performance and enables your computer to run more programs at once. A common frustration amongst computer users is how long it can take to launch programs and switch between them. More RAM equals less waiting.

Hard drive

The hard drive gives you space for data and programs. This can easily be expanded with an additional, external, hard drive. You may be surprised at how quickly it will fill up, if your laptop is your only computer and you're also storing personal data, like music and photos, on it.

Peripherals

Multifunction printer

Even though I find myself using it less these days, I still think it's too early to pronounce the printer dead, especially if you use a multifunction printer like I do.

It's a real space-saver – imagine keeping a printer, scanner, photocopier and fax machine in one office. Mine sits neatly on my desk and is handy when I want to email sketches to my designer. He uses his to archive printed documents. When he receives important letters, for example, he scans them into his computer and recycles the hard copy! We're both on our way to paperless home offices.

External hard drive

External hard drives are great for adding more storage capacity to your computer but they're especially useful for backing up your machine. This is an important process, which you should do regularly – imagine what would happen if your computer crashed and wouldn't restart, or if it was dropped or stolen.

Macs have backing-up software built-in; as do the latest PCs. If not, try SuperDuper! for the Mac and True Image for the PC.

- SuperDuper! | **www.shirt-pocket.com/SuperDuper**
- True Image | **www.acronis.com**

Keyboard and mouse

If you're going to use a laptop, you probably won't get an additional keyboard and mouse. But you should think about it. Lots of time hunched over your laptop screen is no good for your neck and back. With an additional keyboard and mouse, and a stand that raises your laptop to eye-level, you can prevent a lifetime of aches and pains.

Some companies produce keyboards/mice which are ergonomically designed to prevent repetitive strain injury (RSI).

VoIP phones

You can make serious savings on your phone bill by using a VoIP phone. VoIP stands for 'voice over internet protocol' and basically means making calls over the internet rather than your phone line. As such, it's a much cheaper way of making calls (it's sometimes free). And it's the easiest way to set up a second line. The VoIP phone I use is made by a company called IPEVO.

- IPEVO | **www.ipevo.com**

Software

You may already be using many of these programs, so there's no need to splash out when setting up your business. Once it grows you can upgrade to more advanced versions if required. To start, here are the basics. Later we'll look at software (much of it free or very affordable) for when your business is up and running.

Office software

The industry standard in office software is Microsoft Office. If you're trying to save money, try these free alternatives:

- OpenOffice.org | www.openoffice.org
- Google Docs | www.google.com/docs

Both do pretty much everything that Microsoft Office does, and can open and save Microsoft Office files as well.

Web browser

Internet Explorer and Safari both do a good job when it comes to web browsing, as does Firefox. But there's a browser I use that I think is better. It's called Google Chrome and it's faster, more secure and more customisable.

You can add features that will help you do your work and manage your lifestyle. These include features to control your music (without having to switch programs), comparison shop and even change the way your browser looks. It's a free, small download, and it works on Macs and PCs. Its speedy and uncluttered nature makes it particularly good for netbook use.

- Google Chrome | www.google.com/chrome

Email

If you've got Microsoft Office you might use Outlook (or Entourage, as it's called in the Mac version), which is Outlook Express's big sister. It includes calendar and address book features, but it's not free (or cheap). On Macs, Mail is standard.

An alternative is provided by the people who make the Firefox browser. It's called Thunderbird and can do pretty much everything that Outlook can. You can also use it with web-based mail, like Gmail.

- Thunderbird | www.getthunderbird.com

Instant messaging and VoIP

Lots of instant messaging programs also allow you to make video and voice calls. Skype integrates text, voice and video chat. With it you can make free calls to other Skype users and to landline or mobile phones for a small fee, deducted from pay-as-you-go style Skype credit.

You can assign a landline-esque phone number to your Skype account in order to receive calls at your computer, using a VoIP handset, or divert calls to your mobile when out and about.

- Skype | www.skype.com

Support

If you're in need of assistance with anything from hardware set-up to software installation, call in the help of a local IT expert. You may know a neighbour who's a dab hand at technology. If not, check out one of a growing number of companies who send a 'geek' direct to your door.

- Geeks-on-Wheels | www.geeks-on-wheels.com
- KnowHow | www.knowhow.com
- Geek Squad | www.geeksquad.co.uk

On the move

Now that you've found the right technology for your office it's time to take it outside. If you ever get tired of your four walls, it's good to know that it's possible to work elsewhere. With a few simple tips and tricks you can enjoy total flexibility, and work from almost anywhere.

With your computer

If you have a laptop, you pretty much have all you need to work on the move. Almost all laptops come with built-in wireless receivers, so you can hop onto Wi-Fi in public places like coffee shops and libraries. But if you're not sure whether there'll be ample power supply where you're going, a spare battery is well worth considering.

SHOULD I BUY A TABLET COMPUTER OR A LAPTOP?

Like the rest of the world, you've probably been tempted by gorgeous tablet computers like Apple's iPad. But should you buy one instead of a laptop? Can you really get as much business-work done on a tablet?

Well, it really depends on the nature of your business. If you'll be out and about a lot, visiting clients and customers, then buying a tablet becomes a serious consideration. But if your work will involve lots of sitting at a desk or writing long documents, you may find that a tablet PC is not for you. The iPad is constantly improving as a business machine thanks to the App Store, but be prepared to buy an external keyboard to cope with long writing sessions.

The future of computing could lie somewhere between tablets and laptops: ultrabooks. Ultrabooks are really thin, fast laptops. They have traditional features, like a full-size keyboard and trackpad, but usually no DVD drive and limited hard drive storage. That's okay, though, as a lot of your work will take place in the 'Cloud' (more on that later!). Because of their size and weight, ultrabooks are really portable.

Getting connected

You'll need broadband right from the start: during your research, while you're setting up your business, through to when it grows and takes over the world!

Your two main options are ADSL broadband, which is offered by companies like BT, Orange and Sky, and cable broadband from Virgin Media. The biggest difference is that ADSL requires a phone line, while cable broadband does not.

The advantage of cable broadband is that if you don't have a landline phone, and always use your mobile, you can save money by not having to pay line rental on your phone as well as on your internet connection. It's often faster, too, but you'll need to check whether it's available in your area. ADSL broadband is more commonplace and there are lots of companies offering it. As always, read the fine print before you sign anything. Here are some things to look out for:

Price

Some broadband prices seem really cheap but often the prices advertised are for the first few months of an 18-month contract, so make sure you know what you're getting into.

Usage

Some broadband companies will set restrictions on the amount of data you can download in a month and sometimes even charge you extra if you go over your agreed limit. These limits rarely affect most users, but if your business is the kind that needs to send and receive lots of information, look for deals with generous monthly download allowances. Or, better still, unlimited downloads.

Customer support

If you're installing broadband for the first time, you might need some help setting up and, once you're up and running, for what to do when your connection suddenly drops. For these sorts of queries it's handy to have good customer support, so check to see what's on offer and, crucially, how much it should cost to call for help.

Network

Setting up a network used to be the work of professionals and, I suppose, in big companies it still is. But setting one up for your home by yourself is much easier these days.

There are two types of wireless router: one for ADSL internet service providers, like Sky and BT, and another for cable internet, like Virgin Media. Check with your internet service provider to find out which is the best router for your type of connection.

If you didn't get a router from your provider, check out Netgear.

- Netgear | **www.netgear.co.uk**

The Cloud

If you already use web mail, you'll be accustomed to the idea of your messages and contacts being available from any computer or device connected to the internet. So, how about running your entire business from any computer or device anywhere?

The Cloud refers to web apps. You run them through your web browser and all the data is stored online, so in effect you can use them from pretty much any computer anywhere!

The best example is provided by Google, whose Google Apps (**www.google.com/a**) offering includes email, instant messaging, a calendar, word processor, spreadsheet and presentation software, as well as a website builder. It's free and easy to use.

All the work you do is stored in 'The Cloud' so you can log in and out from anywhere and see the same information. Also, if your computer crashes or you buy a new system you won't lose any data or have to reinstall it on a new machine.

TEN FREE CLOUD APPS FOR YOUR BUSINESS

Cloud apps are not only fantastically useful, they don't take up room on your computer and you don't have to worry about backing up your data. They're also, more often than not, free to use.

Here are ten of our favourite free cloud apps for business.

1. Dropbox (**www.dropbox.com**) | Dropbox is like a thumb drive in the sky. It's a folder that sits on your computer, but its contents are stored remotely and synced across other computers and devices that are signed into your Dropbox account. No-nonsense sharing, if you're working with others, and peace of mind that all your work is backed up.

2. Evernote (**www.evernote.com**) | Evernote is a bit like Dropbox, but for your brain. It helps you "remember everything" by allowing you to capture notes and ideas, photos and screen grabs, sounds and links, sync them automatically to the cloud and access them from practically anywhere – great for the planning stages of your business.

3. Google Docs (**docs.google.com**) | As broadband gets quicker and more reliable, Google Docs is becoming a bit of a threat to Microsoft Office. It includes apps for word processing, spreadsheets, presentations, drawings and forms – except all the apps run inside your browser rather than on your desktop. All of your work is stored in the cloud and it's easy to collaborate with others in real time on the same document.

4. Gmail and Google Calendar (**mail.google.com**, **calendar.google.com**) | I've mentioned Gmail before, but did you know Google also make excellent calendar software? Both are really useful if you plan to work on the move.

5. Google Analytics (**www.google.com/analytics**) | When your website is up and running, you'll want to know how many people are visiting. Google Analytics, like most of Google's services, is free, and helps you understand your website statistics, including where your visitors are from, which pages

they visited the most, and how they found your website in the first place.

6. HootSuite (**www.hootsuite.com**) | If social media is part of your marketing plan – and it probably is! – there's no better way to manage your social media presence than with HootSuite. It keeps you on top of your Twitter, Facebook and LinkedIn accounts, as well as what your customers and potential customers are saying about your business.

7. Delicious (**www.delicious.com**) | Delicious is a bookmarking service that keeps all of your important links in the cloud so you can get to them from any computer.

8. Trello (**www.trello.com**) | There's so much to do when starting a business, but you can keep on top of all your tasks with Trello. This is like a Pinterest for tasks and ideas and can be shared with others.

9. Basecamp (**www.basecamp.com**) | If some tasks involve other people and form part of larger projects, check out project management software, Basecamp. It allows you to share files, deliver projects on time and keep communication organised and out of your inbox.

10. MailChimp (**www.mailchimp.com**) | To make sure your business message is in other people's inboxes, put together a newsletter with MailChimp, send it out to your customer mailing list and track its success. Just make sure people have signed up to your mailing list before hitting 'send'!

8. WORKING 5 TO 9

You don't need to give up your studies or throw in the day job to get all this done. Nor do you need to for the next two stages – launch and growth. You can plan the business, register the business and continue to run the business successfully by 'working 5 to 9' – this is the term I apply to the five-million-plus people in the UK who are working or studying by day and building a business at night and weekends.

It's a sensible way to start and grow. If you're working a day job, you give yourself the time to build confidence and cash flow in the business, and can keep putting money aside until you're ready to go full time in your own venture.

Here's what you need to do regarding your current job and boss in order to make this as smooth as possible.

The contract

If you have written terms and conditions of employment they are likely to contain reference to the pursuit of personal business ventures outside your contracted working hours. The clauses to look out for include 'the employee's duties and obligations' and what is commonly known as 'whole time and effort'. These clauses require the employee to devote the whole of their time, attention and abilities to the business of the employer.

If your contract contains these or similar clauses, don't despair, as it doesn't necessarily mean you can't pursue your business. Many employment contracts are drafted using standard templates with little consideration to personal circumstance. You know your job better than anyone, so if you don't think your business venture will affect the way you do your job, it probably won't – and your employer will recognise this. Having checked how things stand in the contract, it's time to talk things through with your boss.

The conversation

Treat it as an amicable and informal conversation to gauge your employer's initial reaction. I asked Patrick Lockton, a qualified lawyer, for his take on the matter and advice on how employees should go about having this conversation:

"When you approach your employer, be prepared to negotiate, be flexible and compromise. If you think it appropriate, make it clear your business venture will in no shape or form affect your ability to do your job or affect your employer's interests. If anything, it will make you a better, more confident and experienced employee and it will not cost your employer a thing."

Patrick goes on to say:

"After having such a conversation, you can do one of two things:

1. if your employer has not expressed any concerns about your intentions and you have no concerns of your own, disclose your intentions to your employer anyway. Treat it as something you want to do for the sake of clarity and for the record, as opposed to something you want their permission for; or

2. if your employer has expressed concerns, try and negotiate a package that you are both happy with. Address their concerns, agree some ground rules and get their permission in writing. Give your employer as much helpful information as possible. If you are going to need some time off or to change your hours then this is the time to bring it up.

"Always take written notes so that you don't forget what was said and so you can remind your employer what was agreed."

So long as you're not competing with your employer or breaching their trust, you shouldn't have any problem at all in pursuing your 5 to 9 ambitions. After all, as Patrick says, your employer benefits from all the new skills you're picking up, and it doesn't cost them a penny in training or resources!

Tilly Walnes, in our next case study, started her business by working 5 to 9 before easing out of the day job into being her own boss full-time . . .

CASE STUDY

NAME: **Tilly Walnes** | BUSINESS: **Tilly and the Buttons**

DIY dressmaker, blogger and author Tilly Walnes started her popular blog, Tilly and the Buttons (**www.tillyandthebuttons.com**), as a New Year's Day dare in 2010.

"I knew absolutely nothing about blogging, apart from the fact that I found blogs, written by real people, so much more authentic and inspiring to read than magazines. At the time I had a day job that I loved, in which I was responsible for nearly all the professional training for independent cinemas and film festivals that took place across the UK and Europe. The reason I started blogging (aside from the fact that I couldn't resist the dare) was that I'd just started making my own clothes for fun and didn't know anyone in real life who shared my passion, so I wanted to connect with the virtual sewing circle I'd discovered online."

In the beginning, Tilly found her first readers by contributing to group blogs and commenting on other sewing blogs.

"As my experience grew, my blog became less random and more purposeful, less about what I was making and more about inspiring and helping other people to start sewing. Thinking from your reader's point of view and providing strong content is key to ensuring people come back for more. Now Tilly and the Buttons is one of the most popular craft blogs in the world, with around half a million views a month."

Tilly's blog started as a 5 to 9 occupation, with Tilly writing away in the evenings and weekends while working full-time.

"It's very labour intensive to make clothes, design projects, photograph tutorials and write posts. Bloggers can get a lot of emails too, so you have to be clear with yourself about which types of enquiries are and aren't worth your time. Many bloggers burn out; it's important to stay inspired, schedule posts in advance, and have a strong understanding of your blog's point of difference so you can stay focused and keep coming up with great content."

As the blog became more of a commitment for Tilly, she started to consider decreasing time in the day job in order to increase time on the blog.

"At first it seemed crazy to leave my film industry career behind, but I was becoming increasingly passionate about making stuff. I was itching to spend more time on Tilly and the Buttons and loved the idea of becoming my own boss. I'm a cautious person so I began by going part-time in my day job and didn't jump ship until I was making the equivalent of a full-time salary each month from the blog and related opportunities. Making the transition gradually meant that handing in my notice at work wasn't at all scary. Oh, and it's the best thing I've ever done!"

Tilly is now generating income from a range of sources.

"I don't keep all my eggs in the same basket. My readers love to discover fabric shops, sewing schools and related businesses, so I have a sponsorship programme on the blog that advertises hand-picked businesses that fit the interests of my audience. Following reader requests to share my garment designs, I launched a small line of stylish dressmaking patterns which are supported by refreshingly clear instructions aimed at beginners. I recently wrote my first book, Love at First Stitch (Quadrille, published May 2014), so the advance on royalties has provided a nice cushion for a while. Plus I teach workshops in partnership with sewing schools and do the occasional paid public speaking gig."

This maker and blogger has also successfully turned her hand to press and promotion, including an appearance on a popular TV show.

"I've had some great press coverage, from being named "Best for DIY Fashion" by Channel4.com to mentions in the *Guardian* and a regular column in *Crafty* magazine. In 2013 I was a contestant on BBC2's *The Great British Sewing Bee*, which awakened the nation's interest to what was previously a very niche hobby. While these incidents have all helped increase the blog's visibility, the most effective form of marketing for me has been to blog strong content regularly – to create posts that I know my readers will love, and to stay on their radar."

Tilly has much to look forward to, with ambitious plans for growth.

'My current priority is to get my sewing patterns printed into lovely packages. I initially launched them as digital downloads for customers to print at home, since I had no idea how popular they'd be and didn't want to invest too much cash in their production before beta testing them and seeing if there was a demand. At the time of writing, I've sold 2,500 patterns and research tells me that printed patterns will sell so much better than digital, so that's what I'm focusing on now. I've already had a few retailers contact me out of the blue to ask if they can stock them, which is a promising sign.

"I'm not turning my back on digital, though, as it allows a very cost-effective and scaleable business model, and has so much potential for engaging people interactively. I'd love to create more digital products this year, probably an e-course or eBook. It's becoming more and more clear that I can't do this all on my own, though, so I'm also plotting how to get more help!"

If you're reading this and think you can lend a hand to this successful and likeable entrepreneur, you know where to find her!

● **www.tillyandthebuttons.com** | **@TillyButtons** | **pinterest.com/TillyButtons**

TOP TIP: "Know your audience and their needs so you can cater for them better than anyone else can, and so they keep coming back for more. This is one of the reasons blogging is so great – my readers also feel like my pals!"

9. STARTING ON A BUDGET AND STRAIGHTFORWARD FINANCE

It has never been more straightforward to build a business on a shoestring of a budget and keep on top of finances with basic spreadsheets or software. You probably already have a computer and a mobile phone, so you might not need to buy much more equipment (depending on your business). Here are some tips for keeping costs low.

Start the business from home

Why take on the cost of an office when the spare room/attic/garden shed will do just as well? Think of the money you'll save: no premises, no commute, no overpriced sandwiches at lunchtime ... !

Embrace social media

Make the most of free or low-cost technology tools to raise your profile and make sales. Chapter 12 offers details of the major social media tools and how they can best be used to your benefit.

Beg, borrow and barter

When starting out, access all the free and discounted resources you can.

THE BEAUTY OF BARTER: Many start-up businesses barter their goods and services, e.g. "I'll produce a sales brochure for you, in exchange for a handmade cushion for my living room." This works well – both parties get what they want. But take heed of the tax implications. Bartering means money doesn't show up in your accounts, but there has been an exchange of goods and services which implies a taxable activity. The taxman could view bartering as a way to avoid tax. Nevertheless, with so many beneficial arrangements underway, maybe it's time they revised the tax situation?

Paula Hutchings, our next case study, benefited from trading skills in getting her business off the ground . . .

CASE STUDY

NAME: **Paula Hutchings** | BUSINESS: **Marketing Vision Consultancy**

Paula Hutchings had been working for major companies marketing well-known household brands in the UK and Australia for over 10 years. When she had children, it was time for a change.

"Once I had my son, I took the opportunity to leave the corporate world behind and follow my long-term dream to run my own business. I set up Marketing Vision Consultancy in 2010 and we relocated back to the UK in July 2012. My main goal was to take the knowledge and experience I'd gained in the corporate world and translate this into affordable solutions for small business owners."

When it came to picking up tips to start her business, Paula took a course in small business essentials which covered areas such as legal, HR, sales, and customer service, and attended Enterprise Nation's StartUp Saturday to meet other start-ups in the same position as her.

"Having worked in brand management, I felt comfortable with running a business, but took courses to ensure I had all bases covered and to get closer to the small business ethos. I also spoke to people I knew who had set up on their own to gain insights about the reality of running a business."

To grow the business, Paula has relied on 'skills-trading' with other professionals and like-minded people.

"My first experience of skills-trading was in Sydney when I first set up the business. I wanted a website but was short of funds so didn't really want to pay for it! I was lucky enough to find a web designer who was willing to build the site in return for marketing support for a business of his. This trade worked out really well. I went on to trade for graphic design work, photography and even haircuts! It helped me to get things I needed for the business when funds were tight, but it also helped me gain valuable experience when I was just starting out. I still skills-trade now if the right opportunity arises. To me it's important to support small businesses and start-ups in the same way that people supported me when I first set up. It's also a great way to make new contacts."

As a marketeer, Paula is well-equipped to carry out her own marketing and feels that blogging and sharing her expertise has been the most effective activity to date.

"Since arriving back in the UK, blogging has become a really valuable marketing exercise for me. I have become a regular guest blogger for Enterprise Nation, and have been approached to write for two other sites. It's been a great way to share my knowledge and experience with small business owners and it's also led to new clients, friendships and some really interesting opportunities. Supported by Twitter, blogging has been the most successful way for me to promote Marketing Vision without any financial investment."

Looking ahead, Paula will be increasingly focused on growing the business. She currently works with clients in the UK and Australia and is starting to connect with businesses in the EU too.

"I will continue to work with and build my existing network of partners in affiliated industries such as web and graphic design to offer clients professional and affordable support. There are some really exciting opportunities in the pipeline."

This growth will come with the help of support that Paula has already relied on.

"I have a mentor, some strong business-minded friends and an amazingly supportive husband who have kept me on track. Having two children has thrown up some challenges but I truly think that as long as you have a viable business idea, with a lot of hard work and determination (and perhaps a little bit of luck along the way!) you can be successful at whatever you set your mind to."

- **www.marketingvision.co.uk** | @MarketingVC

TOP TIP: "Don't underestimate the amount of leg-work it takes to get a business off the ground!"

Make the most of offers

One last tip for keeping costs low at the start: don't forget to visit the Enterprise Nation offers page (**www.enterprisenation.com/partner-offers**) to access deals from top brands.

These tips and techniques will help your budgeting. When it comes to getting hold of funds, there are a number of places to look.

Funding

Friends and family

Friends and family are people you can trust – and asking them for money hopefully won't come with strings attached. Do consider having a written agreement, though, that covers the amount borrowed and a payback schedule.

Start Up Loans

Introduced by the government in 2012, Start Up Loans are made to entrepreneurs across England and Wales. Alongside a loan, you also receive a mentor who offers help throughout your business journey.

Enterprise Nation works closely with Virgin StartUp, a StartUp Loans distribution partner. With Virgin StartUp, you will receive a loan, mentor, discounts from the Virgin group of companies and the opportunity to supply to them too!

- **www.startuploans.co.uk**
- **www.virginstartup.org**

David Galbraith turned to Start Up Loans when he needed some capital to get going and growing. . . .

CASE STUDY

NAME: **David Galbraith** | BUSINESS: **SWIG Flasks**

It was whilst at university that David Galbraith's entrepreneurial streak emerged:

"At university I ran a burrito shop and developed a new brand of beer. This provided the foundation I needed to start my business of branded hip flasks."

During the 2012 Christmas break David spotted a gap in the market for a more desirable hip flask product. One year later his product was well on its way to becoming a Christmas best-seller.

"I was all set to join the graduate scheme at Citigroup but decided to forego the salary, security and monotony to join the New Entrepreneurs Foundation Class of 2013 instead. It matched me with a captain of industry who I got to shadow on placement

for six months, alongside a rigorous foundation training programme on becoming an entrepreneur for life."

As well as support from New Entrepreneurs Foundation, David made connections with StartUp Britain and the British government's Start Up Loans scheme:

"The New Entrepreneurs Foundation provided mentors, coaching and an amazing cohort with whom to work through my plans. StartUp Britain provided my new business, SWIG, a space in the PopUp Britain Piccadilly shop and the Start Up Loans scheme gave me a loan of £10,000 to get the cash-flow-intensive business moving."

David found the Start Up Loan application process straightforward:

"The application process was a short business plan submission followed by a day-long workshop. I originally received £4,500, which was followed by a top up of £5,500 to aid cash flow. We are in a golden age that this support is available and I feel privileged that the application process was slick. It all made sure that needing cash did not hamstring my business."

SWIG is growing; David now has 16 suppliers within the UK who provide various parts of the SWIG product.

"After I get all my supplies in, I am often found processing all the ingredients into the final product. So cutting fabric and glueing packaging together is a normal Saturday night for me. This is something that will be scaled in time, but for my first run of 600 flasks it was well within reach of something I could do myself."

David has now sold the entirety of his first run of flasks and is looking to scale. His efforts at SEO have paid off, with SWIG now appearing as a top result on Google for hip flasks, ahead of eBay, M&S, Aspinal, Etsy and Notonthehighstreet.

"I want SWIG flasks to be one of the top gifts out there. To ensure this happens, I'm going to tighten my supply chain from the ground up and then sell, sell, sell."

- **www.swigflasks.com** | @swigflasks

TOP TIP: "Read lots of case studies about people who have done it or are in the process. It will give you a bank of reference points from other people's success stories that will help you with many of the decisions you make going forward."

Crowd funding

Crowd funding is fast becoming a popular route to secure start-up and follow-on funding. It involves sourcing funds from a crowd of others and there are three main types of it:

1. Reward

This is where people fund your business (or product) in exchange for rewards. Possibly the most well-known site to offer this form of funding is Kickstarter (**www.kickstarter.com**).

2. Equity

This is where people invest in your business in exchange for equity, i.e. a percentage of the business.

3. Loan

This is where you raise a loan and repay with interest.

In raising funds from the crowd, not only do you secure the capital you need, you can also attract attention and an audience of potential customers. As crowd funding has become more popular, the number of crowd funding platforms has increased. The next two pages detail the main platforms and their key terms of business.

The bank

Ask to speak to a small business advisor at your local bank. Take a copy of your business plan with you and be prepared to talk it through.

A CLEAR DIVISION: Open a bank account early on so you don't mix up your business and personal finances, which may complicate record keeping.

PLATFORM	MAX INVESTMENT LEVEL	EQUITY/ LOAN/ REWARD	FEES	KEEP FUNDS IF DON'T HIT TARGET	SECTOR FOCUS
Buzzbnk.org	Suggested amount between £5,000 and £30,000.	Loan and reward	5%	No – money returned to backers.	Social enterprises
Crowdcube.com	No maximum amount	Equity	5% plus £1,750 to cover legal and admin fees.	No – money returned to backers. Automatic deadline of 60 days is set from the day the investment pitch is uploaded.	
Indiegogo.com	Not stated	Reward (referred to as 'perks')	Flexible funding package: pay 9% and receive 5% in return if successfully hit target, i.e. overall fee of 4%. Or fixed funding: pay 4% only if hit target.	Yes – but pay higher fee of 9%.	
Kickstarter.com	No maximum but company states: "the average project is raising around $5,000, but many projects have raised significantly more".	Reward	5% plus payment processing fees of 3–5%.	No – money returned to backers.	
Crowdfunder.co.uk	£50,000	Reward	5% and 3% transaction fees to Go Cardless.	No – money returned to backers.	
Zequs.com		Reward	5%	No – money returned to backers.	Creative projects

Spacehive.com	No maximum amount	Reward	3.75% on first £500,000, 2.5% on the next £500,000 and 1.5% thereafter.	No – money returned to backers.	Community projects and public spaces
Sponsume.com	No maximum amount	Reward	4% on projects that reach target and 9% on projects that don't reach target.	Yes – this platform follows policy of Keep It All as opposed to All or Nothing.	
Unbound.co.uk	No maximum amount	Reward	Publishing	No – money returned to investors if target not met.	Publishing

For more detail on crowd funding and other forms of funding, download the free eBook *50 ways to find funding for your business* in the bookshop at Enterprise Nation: **www.enterprisenation.com/books/50-ways-to-find-funding-for-your-business**

Carol Lovell chose Kickstarter to source funds for her new business . . .

CASE STUDY

NAME: **Carol Lovell** | BUSINESS: **Stow London**

Carol Lovell and Sarah Koche, founders of luxury leather travel gifts company Stow London, met almost a decade ago through their children's nursery.

"Our common interest in addition to the children was business. I was running a business that imported jewellery from Cape Town, and Sarah was starting a business importing leather goods from India. We had much to discuss and always bounced ideas off each other for our individual ventures. In 2009 we first discussed working together and regularly met to review ideas."

Three years and a few meetings later, this entrepreneurial duo came up with a concept and product that would allow them to combine their previous skills and experience in a joint venture. Stow London was officially launched as a luxury leather travel gifts company at the end of September 2013.

"Sarah and I have the same vision for the business but very different roles. We work by agreeing all decisions together but divide the business into key areas of responsibility between us. Sarah has a very strong retail background from years in management at John Lewis so she oversees relationships with online retail partners and is now working on developing our high street presence. She also manages the financial (including pricing) and administrative aspects of the business. My strengths lie with the creative and direct sales side, so I oversee the various creative processes, which includes product design and development, branding, marketing and PR plus our social media activity and e-commerce strategy."

When it came to raising funds, Carol and Sarah opted for crowd funding as they didn't want to take a loan from a bank, nor were they eligible for any government grants or loans.

"We wanted to not only raise funds for a first production run but also raise awareness of the brand in its early stages of development. We knew about Kickstarter and had backed a couple of projects ourselves to see how it worked. We set a target of raising £4,200 – just enough for an initial small production run. We spent four weeks developing the pitch; at the time it was quite stressful as we were so keen for it to be a success. We didn't want to be a failed project on Kickstarter and it didn't help that many of our own contacts didn't know what crowd funding was. People assumed we were asking for equity investment when what we were actually asking for was a pledged sum in exchange for a reward of one of our products at a discount if we hit the target. But I'm delighted to say we raised £5,702 in three weeks!"

One of the biggest contributors came from LinkedIn, as did Stow's introduction to a production partner.

"We were keen to have the products made in the UK but none of the suppliers had the expertise to produce the semi-moulded cases we wanted. We ended up finding a superb partner in Spain via LinkedIn. On meeting the manufacturer in person, we very quickly felt we'd found the right partner and gave him four design specs to produce samples. He was as good as his word, but we also flew with a strong gut feeling about him."

Since that first production run, the company has notched up some strong achievements.

"The plan was to launch online first via our own site and then with www.notonthehighstreet.com, which we did in the same month. The next month we developed partnerships with other online platforms such as www.handpickedcollection.com, www.lux-fix.com and www.shareagift.com. Then we were selected for the exclusive Wolf & Badger boutique in Notting Hill, which only features up and coming designers and brands. Next is attendance at our first trade show at London's Top Draw where we're launching the range to the retail trade. We have contacted 60 retailers to let them know we'll be there so hopefully something will come from that!"

When it comes to marketing, the Stow founders have been careful with their budget, spending time on social media and working on their SEO.

"We have not spent anything on advertising yet – instead we invested in a fashion PR professional recommended by a senior UK retail figure. In the past couple of months her efforts have seen our travel jewellery cases featured in the *FT*'s 'How to Spend It Gift Guide', *YOU Magazine* Christmas gift guide, the *Stylist*'s 'Object of Desire' and in *The Lady Magazine*. As well as press we are focusing on working with relevant travel, style and fashion bloggers."

The co-founders are aiming to achieve the same amount of progress in the next 12 months as they have witnessed in the past year.

"The aim is to consistently build online sales through our website and other online partners whilst developing strong partnerships with key boutiques and stores throughout the UK. We are working on new products and as our designs are non-seasonal gifts for people who love to travel in style, we'll be looking at opportunities around Valentine's Day, Mother's Day, Father's Day etc."

In short, it looks set to be a busy year for Stow London, Sarah and Carol.

www.stowlondon.co.uk | @ stowlondon1

TOP TIP: "If you want to do it, if you believe in it – say yes and don't let anyone tell you it can't be done. Find a way."

Shelling out the funds

Apply to the Shell LiveWIRE Grand Ideas Awards to be in with a chance of winning £1,000. Four awards are made each month to anyone aged 16 to 30 who is starting a business in the UK or within their first 12 months of trading.

www.shell-livewire.org/awards

See later for more details on Shell LiveWIRE and other awards to enter.

Investors

Angel investors and venture capitalists can help raise large amounts of start-up funding or development capital for businesses looking to grow. It might be an idea to consider this route further down the line. It doesn't have to be a gruesome experience (à la *Dragons' Den*), though, as there are plenty of funds and investors out there who are eager to part with their money and back good ideas. What's more, the government has made it financially attractive for angels to invest through the Seed Enterprise Investment Scheme which offers individual income tax relief of 50% and exemption from capital gains tax (CGT) on any proceeds of sale of a SEIS investment.

Visit the dedicated SEIS website (**www.seis.co.uk**) for details and the Business Finance For You site (**www.businessfinanceforyou.co.uk**), which offers a listing of available grants and funds, searchable by your local area.

In the words of an Angel

Andy Yates is an experienced angel investor and serial entrepreneur. In terms of what he looks for, he says:

"Great businesses are created by great people. I always look out for the three Ps – passion, personality and perseverance. I also back entrepreneurs who really listen and learn. The ability to be flexible, take on board advice and feedback and adapt a product or service to win customers is the real key to unlocking success."

- Angels Den | **www.angelsden.co.uk**
- Funding Circle | **www.fundingcircle.com**
- Find Invest Grow | **www.findinvestgrow.com**
- Springboard | **www.springboard.com**
- UK Business Angels Association | **www.bbaa.org.uk**

See later for details on accelerator programmes that will take your business from start to growth at speed, and often come attached with funding.

Straightforward finance

When planning a business you'll want to be sure earnings are higher than outgoings. Earnings are also referred to as revenue, turnover or income and this should be a greater figure than outgoings, overheads or costs. Let's look at the items that come within each category.

Incoming

Earn from selling your product or service and any associated income opportunities. For example, you set up a business selling unique handmade cushions. From the outset, earn income from:

- Selling 24 x handmade cushions at £25 per cushion = £600 income per week

- Speaking at events to teach others how to make cushions = £150 per event

- Custom requests, e.g. a unique and one-off production = £75 per item

- Developing a blog on the topic of cushions that attracts cushion-istas as readers and paying advertisers as your customers – £priceless!

Outgoings

Here are the costs; some payable at start-up stage and others ongoing:

- **Salary** – how much do you need to pay yourself? (You will be pleasantly surprised at how thriftily you can live when not commuting.)

- **Property** – start the business from home and avoid the cost of a pricey office.

- **Raw materials and equipment** – what are the materials you need to deliver and promote your finished cushions? And do you need any equipment to make that product; a sewing machine, computer, printer, smartphone or camera?

- **Insurance** – be insured from the start and choose a policy that covers all your needs.

- **Website/promotion materials** – we will cover in Chapters 10–12 how you can build a home on the web and promote the business on a shoestring of a budget.

Keep records of 'Incoming' and 'Outgoing' in a basic Excel spreadsheet as in the following. See later for an example invoice and how to keep a record of invoices raised and amounts paid.

INCOMING

Product sales	£xx
Sponsorship/Advertising	£xx
Other contracts	£xx

OUTGOINGS

Salary	(£xx)
IT	(£xx)
Office	(£xx)
Raw materials/equipment	(£xx)
Insurance	(£xx)
Marketing & promotion	(£xx)
Other	(£xx)

PROFIT	**£XX**

II. LAUNCH

You have your idea. It's supported by research and a plan pointing you in the right direction. You've sorted out all the technology you need to get going. And with the company registered, it's time to get into business by making sales and some noise.

66 Be a sponge: absorb as much help and support as you can! Approach others. Listen. Join a networking group. All too often I see entrepreneurs over-protective of their venture. They miss vital guidance. **99**

– Claire Young, founder, School Speakers

10. CREATE A FIRST IMPRESSION

You may have started out by making sales to friends and family who know and trust you to deliver. To attract new customers, it's important to create the right first impression, whether that customer meets you at an event or visits your home on the web. Here's guidance to getting it right and offering a professional welcome.

Your home on the web

You have the tools and connection to get online. The first thing to do is build a presence through a blog, website or store. Not only is a website your window to the world and home on the web, it has become an essential requirement for any new business. Your site can be used as a powerful marketing tool and a way to make money. Having the right technology and knowledge allows you to build, develop and maintain your site. And you can do it all in-house.

Let's look at the three main ways to develop a professional-looking online presence.

1. Blogging

Blogging is a website or part of a website that's regularly updated by an individual or a group of bloggers. There are blogs on any number of topics and the fact that anyone can start blogging for free makes the medium diverse and exciting.

It's an easy way to get online, as you write posts on your topic of choice, upload images and video, and become the go-to place for customers looking for your advice/tips/services/products. Search engines love blogs and the more you write, the higher up the search-engine ranks you will go. Writing regularly is likely to lead to a loyal readership and it's an effective way to communicate your news with existing and potential customers. Readers can add their comments to your entries if you allow them, and you can use your blog to answer questions and establish yourself as an expert in your field.

- Blogger | **www.blogger.com**
- Typepad | **www.typepad.com**
- WordPress | **www.wordpress.com**

See Chapter 11 for details on how to make money from your blog.

Now you see me

After getting to grips with blogging, why not try your hand at vlogging? This stands for video blogging and is an effective way to interact with customers who want to see you, your products and other happy customers. Vlogging expert, Niamh Guckian, offers tips on how to vlog like a pro:

VLOG HOW-TO

"Vlogging can help you tell people your story: a demonstration of your skills, an atmosphere piece, or an interview.

THE GEAR: "Become an expert on your chosen camera, whether a phone or something fancier.

"Where possible use manual control with your camera – this applies to white balance, exposure and focus. Learn the rules and *then* have fun breaking them.

"Use focus and depth of field to add style to your shooting. Using a tripod sets your work apart from amateur shooting and allows for good steady shot composition.

SAFETY: "Using a small camera can make you feel like you can take risks that you wouldn't otherwise. This has advantages at times but don't take unnecessary risks. Don't shoot from rooftops or get into water!

LIGHT: "As a video-blogger, you will mostly be working with available or natural light. Try to get the most from what's available at the time.

SOUND: "Audio recording is a specialist art form. What we need to achieve as self-shooters is clean and non-distorted sound. Distorted audio is not fixable, and can usually be prevented.

INTERVIEWS: "If your piece is interview-based, engage with the contributor, communicate with them and let them know clearly what you want them to do. Create an atmosphere where the contributor is comfortable, and make sure they know they can stop and start again, or ask questions.

"Make sure the interview is a sequence, that it has a beginning, middle and end, and can stand alone if necessary.

EXPORT AND UPLOAD: "Learn about the optimum settings and platforms for your finished piece."

2. Your own website.

Build your own website that you can spec to your own requirements or invest in a template website. Let's look at both options.

DIY

You have decided to build your own site or have a developer take care of it for you.

The first thing to do is buy a domain. A domain makes up a part of your website and email address. So, for example, the domain name I own is enterprisenation.com. My website address is **www.enterprisenation.com** and my email address is **emma@enterprisenation.com**. Both use the enterprisenation.com domain name.

A domain isn't only your address on the web, it's also a big part of your brand, so think carefully when choosing one. There are domain registration companies whose websites allow you to check for available domain names and often suggest available alternatives.

You could consider a .CO domain for your business as it is boundary-less and you also benefit from access to .CO membership which comes with free support on Search Engine Optimisation. See **www.enterprisenation.com/offers** for details.

Registering a domain name doesn't give you a website, just an address for it (and an email address). Think of it like reserving a car parking space. You've got the space, now you need to buy the car!

A hosting company will sort you out with the web space to host your site. This is measured in megabytes and gigabytes, just like the information on your computer.

In terms of how much web space you will need, basic hosting packages offer about 250 MB of space, but anything over 1 or 2 GB is more sensible and will also allow you to handle more traffic as your website grows more popular.

With a domain name and web space, potential customers should be able to type your website address into their browser and find out all about your business – just as soon as you've built your site. Finding a hosting company shouldn't be hard. Most domain registration companies, including those mentioned above, offer web space as a package; and hosting companies usually offer domain registration, too.

1&1 Internet Ltd
www.1and1.co.uk

123-reg
www.123-reg.co.uk

GoDaddy
www.godaddy.com

When it comes to hiring a designer, have a think about what you'd like your website to do for your business. The easiest way to start is to think of your website as a brochure, but remember to include the following pages at the very least.

PAGES TO INCLUDE

- **About us:** the story behind your business and its mission.

- **News:** the latest and greatest of your products, business developments, maybe a topical focus if relevant to your business.

- **Products or services:** punchy with the detail, using images of your best work, and text and video testimonials from satisfied customers.

- **FAQs:** questions which you get asked. A lot.

- **Contact us:** email and social media details.

Choose a designer who has carried out work you like the look of and for companies in a similar kind of sector to your own. That way, the designer will understand what site you're after – and what your kind of visitor will be looking for, as well as how they like to browse and buy.

BRIEF A WEB DESIGNER/DEVELOPER

Here's Emily Hewett's (**www.birdsontheblog.co.uk**) advice on how best to brief a web designer/developer:

"WHO ARE YOU? Give a short summary of who you are and what you do. This will help the designer tune in to your particular sector. You'll also need to tell them about your market and how you fit into the larger scheme of things – e.g. competitors, local and national.

"WHAT DO YOU WANT TO ACHIEVE? For example: data capture, sales generation, footfall increase, etc.?

"WHO ARE YOU TALKING TO? Outline a profile of your customer. Who are you targeting? Break it down in terms of sex, age, average income and location.

"WHAT TONE ARE YOU USING? Deciding on how you speak to your audience is important. You may be writing the copy yourself or you may have a copywriter to do this for you. In this section of the brief tell the designer if it's a laid-back chatty tone or formal. The tone of the copy needs to be reflected in the design.

"WHAT ARE YOUR LIKES AND DISLIKES? Provide examples wherever possible. It might be a certain colour palette or illustration style or it could be a format. Any of these things help the designer understand what you're looking for.

"ARE THERE ANY MANDATORY ELEMENTS? Fonts, colours, logos, legal text, images, etc. This way they can make sure they produce something on-brand, adhering to your corporate image.

"WHAT'S YOUR BUDGET? A good designer won't take a large budget and fit a job to it. They should find the most cost-effective way of producing exactly what you want. But if you have a small budget, the designer will have to make decisions based on that.

"WHEN DO YOU WANT IT? Make sure the deadline is clear.

"HAVE YOU COVERED EVERYTHING? Show the brief to a colleague or friend to see if they understand it. Once happy, send or talk it through with your designer and invite questions so they are aware you are approachable and that you are both working from the same list of requirements.

Template sites and payment systems

If DIY feels and sounds too much like hard work, there are a number of companies offering template websites that come with domain registration, hosting, e-commerce and a basic level of design as part of the package – over the page there's a comprehensive list of template site providers offering websites that can be set up today and trading tomorrow. Many e-commerce platform sites come with an in-built payment system; here are the main ones:

PayPal

PayPal has more than 100 million active registered accounts and is available in 190 markets, meaning you can successfully trade in all these markets!

The company offers three main products: website payments standard, website payments pro and express checkout. To enable your customers to buy multiple items, use a free PayPal shopping cart. To put the 'Add to Cart' button on your website you simply copy and paste the HTML code from PayPal to the coding of your own site (**bit.ly/blxrUn**). Your customers then click the button to make a purchase. With PayPal, there are no set-up charges, monthly fees or cancellation charges, and fee levels vary depending on the volume of sales.

Google Checkout

Google Checkout (**checkout.google.co.uk**) is a global payment system. There are no set-up charges and fees depend on the volume of your sales. With monthly sales of less than £1,500, the fee is currently 3.4% plus 20p per transaction. This transaction fee decreases in line with sales volumes increasing.

Sage Pay

Sage Pay (**www.sagepay.com**) is a card payment service that allows you to accept payments by PayPal and major debit and credit cards. It is simple to manage and easy to integrate within your website. The fee is £20 per month for merchants processing up to 1,000 transactions per quarter and 10p per transaction for merchants processing more than 1,000 transactions per quarter, with a minimum charge of £20 per month. There are no set-up fees, no percentage fees and no annual charges.

Stripe

Accept payments from major international debit and credit cards with Stripe (**www.stripe.com**), which charges 2.4% + 20p per successful charge, or less based on volume. Anything you earn via your website is transferred to your bank account on a daily basis. Setting up a Stripe account takes only moments, allowing you to start trading with immediate effect.

Enterprise Nation particularly recommends Moonfruit as a website builder. You can access a special start-up offer from Moonfruit at: **www.enterprisenation.com/offers**

ACTINIC (WWW.ACTINIC.CO.UK)	Actinic Express. £1 set-up fee and £15 per month thereafter for the bronze and basic package.	Company has been established in UK since 1996 and has built a solid reputation. Free 30-day trial on offer.
BIG CARTEL (WWW.BIGCARTEL.COM)	It's free to present five products, with monthly packages increasing to $29.99 per month for displaying up to 300 products.	With its strapline 'Bringing Art to the Cart', US-based Big Cartel has a focus on providing online stores for clothing designers, record labels, jewellers and crafters.
CREATE (WWW.CREATE.NET)	Packages start from £2.99 per month. 30-day free trial available.	Set up your site in minutes and benefit from email support plus online forums.
CUBECART (WWW.CUBECART.COM)	From free to a one-time payment of £84, depending on the features required. Free 30-day trial on offer.	E-commerce shopping cart used by more than one million store owners – so they must be doing something right!
MOONFRUIT (WWW.MOONFRUIT.COM)	A basic site is free to build, moving up to £22.50 per month for premium options.	Moonfruit Shopbuilder automatically creates a store on Facebook and a mobile version of your site.
MRSITE (WWW.MRSITE.COM)	Three packages: £24.99 Beginner, £39.99 Standard, £99.99 Professional	You can buy the product in boxed or email format. Helpful tips on how to start via the site.
OSCOMMERCE (WWW.OSCOMMERCE.COM)	Free	An open source solution with, to date, over 76,000 add-ons available for free to customise your store and increase sales.
SQUARESPACE (WWW.SQUARESPACE.COM)	A standard package is $8 per month, increasing to $24 per month for the business package.	You select a template, start a free trial and get a free domain.
SUPADUPA (SUPADUPA.ME)	Price packages start free and then move through Plankton ($19 per month), Cod ($29 per month) and Caviar ($99 per month).	'Boutique e-commerce for creative minds' comes with the promise these sites will be easy to use and stylishly display your goods. You could spend a while on the main site browsing through what are beautiful looking boutiques.
WEEBLY (WEEBLY.COM)	A free package offers all you need to create a site, including free hosting, or you can opt for the $25-per-month business option with e-commerce built in.	Manage your site on the go via the Weebly app.
WIX (WWW.WIX.COM)	A free build-your-site service with the ability to upgrade to premium plans that start at £10 per month.	Hundreds of designs to choose from and a drag and drop system to get you started.

MAKE YOUR WEBSITE LEGALLY COMPLIANT

These tips are offered by Joanna Tall, founder of
www.OfftoseemyLawyer.com

1. DISPLAY TERMS OF USE

"Think of your website like a board game you are about to play with your visitors. They arrive and are ready to play and you need to state the rules or else it will be chaos! So, for example, state what they can and cannot do – e.g. may they copy your materials? May they link to you? May they rely on the information you provide without double-checking with you or elsewhere? What liability are you prepared to accept? Provide a link to your terms of use, ideally on every page of your website or under a 'Legals' section.

2. DISPLAY YOUR PRIVACY POLICY

"Most websites collect personal data on their visitors either by getting them to register on the site or sign up for a newsletter. By law you must tell visitors what you will be doing with this data and the best way to do this is to set out the information in a privacy policy. Again, a link to it on every page is best. More complex rules apply if you plan to collect sensitive information or information from children, or want to pass the information to third parties; for this you should consult a lawyer. Additionally, you are likely to need to register as a data processor under the Data Protection Act. Simply go to **www.ico.gov.uk** for more information.

3. IF SELLING GOODS OR SERVICES ONLINE, DISPLAY YOUR TERMS OF SALE

"Just as with the board game example, you need rules for selling your goods or services. Most importantly, you need to get your visitors to acknowledge that they accept them. So ideally get them to tick a box stating that they accept them before they proceed to check out. You also need to draw their attention to their rights under the Distance Selling Regulations, e.g. cancellation rights amongst others.

4. PROTECT YOUR COPYRIGHT IN THE WEBSITE CONTENT

"Although you automatically own the copyright in the content that you create, best practice is to remind your visitors! Say, for example: "Copyright 20xx Lawyers R Great Ltd". And if your logo or name is trademarked, broadcast the fact! After all, you will have spent money in getting it that far and it will enhance your brand in the market.

5. STATE WHO YOU ARE!

"By law you need to state a full postal address and contact number and if you are a limited company, the company's registered address, number and country of registration. This also applies to your emails."

Distance Selling Regulations

One thing to bear in mind when selling goods or services to consumers via the internet, mail order or by phone, is compliance with the Consumer Protection (Distance Selling) Regulations 2000. The key features of the regulations are:

- You must offer consumers clear information including details of the goods or services offered, delivery arrangements and payment, the supplier's details and the consumer's cancellation rights before he or she buys (known as prior information). This information should be provided in writing.

- The consumer has a period of seven working days from delivery of the items to cancel their contract with you.

These regulations only apply when selling to consumers, as opposed to businesses. In the event of a contract being ceased, you have to refund money, including delivery charges, within 30 days of the date of cancellation.

- Distance Selling Regulations | **dshub.tradingstandards.gov.uk**

3. A presence on other sites

Maybe you'd prefer to start raising your profile and making sales via other established platform sites, as opposed to your own. Whether selling homemade crafts or business concepts, there are a number of options.

The upside is that these sites attract customers on your behalf, and some of them attract customers from all over the world. Here are seven sales platforms that enable you to sell:

Alibaba

Having a presence on this site enables you to buy and sell with, and source supplies from, companies across the globe. The site has visitors from 240 countries and regions, with over 1 million registered users in the UK. Through the site you can locate suppliers or make sales of your finished product direct to customers. Alibaba is a champion of international trade; carrying out research on the topic, providing a platform for traders to interact, and promoting overseas sales as a form of business that is wholly viable, regardless of company size.

- www.alibaba.com | @AlibabaTalk_UK

Amazon Marketplace

You may be used to buying from Amazon, but have you considered the site as a platform from which to sell? Have your products appear before millions of customers all around the world by signing up to Amazon Marketplace. It offers two sales options: a package for casual sellers who expect to sell less than 35 items a month (a fixed fee per sale plus a referral fee), and, for more seasoned sellers, there is the 'sell a lot' package, which has a monthly charge plus a referral fee for unlimited sales that do not have to be in the Amazon catalogue.

- www.amazon.co.uk/marketplace

eBay

In 2012 there were 190,000 registered businesses trading on eBay in the UK, generating billions of pounds-worth of sales. Having a store on eBay means you are opened up to an international audience and a lot of potential customers.

- www.eBay.co.uk

EBAY EXPERTISE

*Dan Wilson (**www.wilsondan.co.uk**) is an eBay author and co-editor of Tamebay, the highly popular eBay blog. Dan offers five tips on how to make the most of the mega marketplace:*

1. START SMALL

"Go slow until you've found your way. Start with a few, easy-to-post items and learn about eBay before boosting your range and prices. Don't stake too much on your first eBay bet.

2. SELL LIKE YOU MEAN IT

"The eBay marketplace is competitive and you'll lose out unless you have top-notch listings. Craft fabulous item titles, make impeccable pictures and write descriptions that tempt buyers. Be truthful and honest and look professional from the start.

3. BE QUICK OFF THE MARK

"Buyers have come to expect great service. Dispatch orders quickly — preferably within 24 hours of payment — and well packed, and make sure you reply to emails and other communications swiftly, too. The quality and speed of your replies and dispatches has an impact on customer feedback.

4. PUT A LID ON POSTAL COSTS

"Understand postage and packaging costs and make sure you factor it in to your costs where necessary.

5. LOYALTY MEANS PROFIT

"When you're building your eBay business, encouraging repeat buyers is important. Once a buyer trusts you as an online seller, they're likely to keep coming back. Offer discounts and incentives with every dispatch and cross-market complementary products."

Etsy

With its tag line 'Your place to buy and sell all things handmade' this is still the mother of all craft sites. Since the company launched in June 2005, more than 500,000 sellers from around the world have opened up Etsy shops and buyers of Etsy-listed products span more than 150 countries.

To start selling on Etsy you need to register for an account (this requires a credit card and valid email address for verification purposes) and then it costs 20 cents to list an item for four months. When your item sells, you pay a 3.5% transaction fee. For anyone who makes handmade items, the power of this global platform cannot be denied. Head a few pages on for a listing of handmade marketplaces you can try today.

- www.etsy.com | @etsy

Facebook

With more than 1 billion users across the globe and 30 million in the UK, a significant number of your present and potential customers spend time on Facebook every single day. If your business isn't there, it's missing out. Countless small business owners in the UK use Facebook to quickly and cost-effectively grow their company. The easiest way to start is through having an effective Facebook Page. Learn how to do this step by step in the free guide *Boost your Business with Facebook*, which also shows how to connect with new fans and make the most of Facebook ads.

- *Boost Your Business with Facebook* | www.enterprisenation.com/books

iTunes

If you are a creator of audiobooks, a publisher of podcasts or developer of apps, then the iTunes platform is your route to market. For apps, Apple gives 70% of revenues to the seller. Over 60 billion apps have been downloaded from its App Store, making it the world's largest mobile application platform. Become a registered Apple developer for the iPhone (**developer.apple.com/iphone**) submit audio books to iTunes via Audible.com (**www.audible.com**) and create iBooks for the iPad through the iBookstore. Apple is opening up a world of opportunity for content creators and app developers.

- **www.apple.com/itunes**

Enterprise Nation Marketplace

Small business network, Enterprise Nation has launched its own marketplace to match small businesses with talented professionals and advisers. If you're a supplier of advice on sales and marketing, making the most of digital technologies, access to finance etc., create a profile and be matched with small business owners looking for the advice you offer.

- **www.enterprisenation.com/marketplace**

HANDMADE marketplaces

A growing number of sites are dedicated to helping the young artisan and handmade business owner sell goods across the globe.

Etsy – www.etsy.com

"The world's handmade marketplace" (and a great place to start your selling).

How does it work?

1. You list the item on Etsy for a fee. It costs 20 cents (roughly 12p) to list an item for four months.

2. Shoppers then find your item, and purchase it from you directly, using your payment system which you have set up with Etsy. Etsy takes a 3.5% transaction fee from the total price of each sale.

3. You then ship the item directly to your customer.

Getting started

Setting up a shop on Etsy is easy and should only take a few minutes:
www.etsy.com/join

You will need to enter your Etsy username here, which will be displayed to customers looking at your products. Remember to think about your branding and how you want to present yourself to potential customers when entering these details.

Paying fees

All of your fees will be paid using the credit card you list when you register, or the PayPal account you link to your Etsy account. Etsy will calculate your fees on a monthly basis and email you with a list of payments that are due. You can also pay your bill manually through your account.

Community

Etsy has a thriving community where sellers, artists and creators all come together to share their work and ideas with one another. Etsy also run events such as Craft Nights, which could be a great way to meet other crafters and promote your products to a receptive audience.

The site has a blog which highlights new product launches and new initiatives, plus featured sellers and debates on various topics. Forums feature strongly on the site.

Not On The High Street — www.notonthehighstreet.com

"One basket, hundreds of unique shops"

How does it work?

Not On The High Street offers you the chance to promote and sell your product under the umbrella of their brand and be supported by their in-house team. They look after all of the e-commerce, administration and marketing elements of selling through the site, so all you need to worry about are the products.

Not On The High Street differs from a number of other platform sites in that they are very selective about who sells with them and decline over 90% of applications. Membership packages vary but the basic package allows you to add 30 products to your own store, with your own logo, company name and URL.

Getting started

If you're interested in getting set up with NOTHS, you will need to take some photographs of your products and submit these using the online application form.

Applications can take up to seven working days to be processed. After that time you will be contacted by a member of the team.

Folksy – www.folksy.com

"Folksy is a place to buy handmade things, and for makers to sell their work and find supplies. Based in the UK, Folksy aims to reclaim craft and showcase talented makers and their work."

You can sell craft supplies on Folksy as well as handmade goods, so long as they are listed as 'supplies' and not in the 'handmade' category.

How does it work?

1. There are two packages available; the basic package which costs 15p to list an item plus 6% sales commission, and Folksy Plus, which is £45 per year and comes with no listing fees and 6% sales commission.

2. Shoppers purchase from you directly, using your payment system which you have set up with Folksy, for example PayPal, or you can accept other payments, such as cash or cheques at your own discretion. Folksy takes a 6% commission fee from the total value of each sale.

3. You then ship the item directly to your customer.

Getting started

The first thing you need to do is decide on the username for your shop. This can't be changed so think carefully about your branding and how you want to appear to prospective customers.

Once your item is listed, customers can start viewing and purchasing. When an order is received you will get an order from Folksy with all the buyer's details and the information about the product ordered. You will also receive notification to say payment has been completed. You then ship the product directly to the customer.

Paying fees

You settle fees through the Your Account section of the website. The total shown will be made up of billed and unbilled fees as well as the 5% commission on sales.

Community

Folksy features a blog which gives updates on important news and events. The site also has a forum where members can discuss craft tips, as well as events, ideas for your shopfront and anything else that takes your fancy!

DaWanda — en.dawanda.com

"DaWanda is the place for unique and individual products and people. Buy handmade and hard to find goods, share your discoveries with your friends and create your own collections."

How does it work?

List your items on the site and set up your own shop which gives you the option of a direct URL – nice and easy to promote to your customers!

People will browse your listings and when someone orders a product you receive an email. You check the details of the order, making a note of any special requests from the buyer, and once happy to go ahead you click to confirm the order, so the buyer can see the final price and pay you. You then ship the item directly to the customer using the method you have specified in the listing.

Getting started

With DaWanda you can set up your own shop for free – all you need to do is provide a name and set up shop categories. You can create your own shop window at this stage to show off the key items in your shop. As soon as this has been established, you can start listing your items and selling to customers!

DaWanda also features something called the DaWanda widget, a tool for displaying your shop on your own website or blog.

Paying fees

DaWanda charges a 5% commission on all sales but does not charge for listing products. Once your fees reach €5, DaWanda will email you an invoice with instructions on how to pay.

Community

The website features the News Bulletin Board as well as a blog, ideal for getting all the latest information on what DaWanda offers and what's popular on the site. The forums are a great place to chat with other crafters and there are also video, social media and Gift Detective areas.

ArtFire – www.artfire.com

"The Premier handmade marketplace to buy and sell handmade crafts, supplies, vintage and art"

How does it work?

Set up your shop and list as many items as you want, with up to 10 photographs per item.

The customer will browse your shop and place an order. You receive the customer's payment and also their delivery details in order to ship the product.

Getting started

You can set up your shop for free at **www.artfire.com/signup**.

You then pay nothing for 30 days, and after that the rate is $12.95 a month for unlimited listings. ArtFire does not take a commission on sales.

Paying fees

Fees will be taken from your nominated payment card on the same day each month (the one on which you originally signed up). For example, if you joined on the 5th December, you would be charged your monthly fee on the 5th of every month.

Community

ArtFire has a range of different community options for you to get involved in and interact with other members. There are forums where you can communicate and share ideas with other crafters, as well as ArtDaily, which is an opportunity to learn new crafts and get sound business advice, plus there's the chance to join a guild and earn a guild badge, as well as listen to a weekly podcast giving tips on how to promote your business and use ArtFire to its full potential.

MISI (Make It, Sell It) — www.misi.co.uk

"The home of buying and selling handmade in the UK"

How does it work?

Create a shop with MISI and list your items for free. When you sell a product you will receive an email notification from MISI which will prompt you to log in to see the full details of the sale. Payment can either be by cheque or PayPal, and once payment is received, you ship the product direct to the customer.

Paying fees

MISI charges 20p per listing, which will be added to your account as soon as you start listing items. MISI also take a 3% commission fee on every sale and this is also added to your account. Fees are then payable on a monthly basis.

Community

The MISI community section is broken down into several areas including: a blog where crafters write about their latest ideas, materials and events; a forum for sharing tips and ideas; and a Meet the Maker section where shop-owners and crafters are encouraged to share their experiences with the community.

A TOP QUALITY IMAGE: Whether you decide to start online with a blog or a full e-commerce site, place high quality images on your site and printed materials so that on first click or at first glance, a customer is inclined to buy. Take professional images yourself or consider subscribing to a stock image library such as **www.istock photo.com**. Other image libraries include: **www.imagesource.com**, **www.photos .com** and **www.gettyimages.com**. Search for Creative Commons licensed images you can use commercially from Flickr at **www.compfight.com**.

Rise up the search engine ranks

Promote your business and website through search engine optimisation. Commonly referred to as SEO, this is the process by which you can improve rankings for your website in the top search engines such as Google, so that your site appears on the first few pages of results rather than on page 75.

Google is a search engine that uses software known as 'spiders' to crawl the web on a regular basis and find sites to add to their index. There are steps you can take to make it easier for the spiders to find and add your site.

THINK LIKE A BUYER: When thinking of the keywords to use in PPC (pay per click) ad campaigns (and in search engine optimisation) think of the words your buyers will be using when searching for your product or service. Use the Google AdWords Keyword Tool to find out the most popular search terms. Apply these words in the campaign and include them in the text on your site.

Start with the homepage

Provide high-quality, text-based content on your pages – especially your homepage. If your homepage has useful information and good quality, relevant text, it's more likely to be picked up by the spiders. Beyond the homepage, write pages that clearly describe your topic/service/product. Think about the words users would type to find your pages and include them on the site.

Make contributions

Identify influential bloggers and sites in your trade/industry, contact them and offer to write posts. You can also improve your visibility by writing helpful comments in forums and on other people's posts.

Be well-connected

Improve the rank of your site by increasing the number of other high-quality sites that link to your pages; these are referred to as inbound links. For example, if you're running a competition, go to sites that promote competitions and add yours.

Register your site with the major search engines.

- Google | www.google.co.uk/addurl
- Yahoo! | search.yahoo.com/info/submit
- Bing | www.bing.com/webmaster/submitsitepage.aspx

SEARCH ENGINES LOVE LINKS: Another way to increase your ranking in the search results is to link to other sites and vice versa, but think quality here as opposed to quantity. Sites offering the best 'link juice' are trusted domains, such as news sites, and very popular sites. You could post comments on such sites and blogs and include a link back to your site. Try these handy hints: approach sites complementary to your own and suggest reciprocal links; ensure that your website link is included in all your social media profiles; register with the major search engines (see above); add your domain to local search services such as Google Maps, Qype, Yahoo! Local and BView.

- **www.google.co.uk/maps**
- **www.yelp.co.uk**
- **www.uk.local.yahoo.com**

Tagging

A webpage's title, referred to as a 'title tag', is part of the SEO mix and can make a difference to your search rankings. It is also the text that appears in the top of the browser window. Include in your title tag the main key phrase you'd like the search engines to associate with your webpage and keep it to 60-90 characters in length. Duncan Green of Moo Marketing is an SEO expert and explains: "the title tag on the homepage for Moo Marketing reads: 'Moo Marketing – Search Engine Marketing –

PPC Management – Search Engine Optimisation'. As you can see the title element is 85 characters long, contains three key phrases and identifies the subject of the webpage."

Pay per click advertising

The results from your efforts in SEO will appear on the main engines as a natural or 'organic' search result. But have you spotted results on the right of the page when searching for items yourself? These are paid-for results and referred to as pay per click or PPC advertising. PPC is where you pay to have ads displayed when people type in certain words, in the hope it will attract more visitors to your site.

Google AdWords is a form of PPC advertising. Think of the key words or phrases you reckon your customers will be searching for and apply them in your Google campaign. Link to your homepage or other pages on the site where you're running a promotion and make the most of geotargeting, which lets you target your ads to specific territories and languages. You are in full control of the budget and campaign duration.

- adwords.google.co.uk

Spread the word

Make it easy for visitors to spread word of your site through social sharing. Have your site Tweeted, Pinned and Liked and make the most of this viral effect. You can add these social bookmarking tools by visiting AddThis (www.addthis.com) and choosing the icons you'd like to have displayed on your site.

Your business in print

Print is far from dead, so get yourself some business cards, postcards and promotion flyers to hand out at business events, social occasions, and to just about anyone you meet! Have fun with designing your cards at www.moo.com and get a range of designs printed in each batch. Sell vintage fashion? Upload pictures of your products to the reverse of each card. Offer web design services? Have a portfolio of sites you've designed there.

Look at my logo!

When you contact potential customers you'll want them to read about you and get a sense of your style. You can do this very effectively with a nice-looking logo or company design that's repeated across all your promotion materials, from business cards to brochures.

Think about what you'd like as your company font, colours and layout. Have a go at designing this yourself or hire the services of a designer/neighbour/friend. Good presentation can make a world of difference. This may just be the difference you need to clinch a contract.

Find a professional to design your logo via these sites:

- Enterprise Nation Marketplace | www.enterprisenation.com/marketplace
- CrowdSPRING | www.crowdspring.com
- 99designs | www.99designs.com
- Concept Cupboard | www.conceptcupboard.com
- Fiverr | www.fiverr.com

Office address

If you are running the business from home there are a couple of reasons why you might not want to put the home address on your business card: it might sound too domestic, and you might not want people turning up on your doorstep!

You can solve this with a P.O. Box number, which starts at £185 per year and is easily set up with Royal Mail (www.royalmail.com/pobox). Alternatively, you could invest in a virtual office, which gives you a more tailored and personal service than a P.O. Box – plus you get a nice-sounding address and a place to use for meetings. Having a virtual office enables you to choose the address that suits you best, have post delivered to that location, and then forwarded on to you. Companies providing this service include:

- Regus | www.regus.co.uk
- Bizspace | www.bizspace.co.uk
- Mail Boxes Etc | www.mbe.co.uk

When holding meetings, consider hiring professional meeting space. Many offer serviced addresses and secretarial services too, so there could be great continuity for your clients if they only have to remember one address.

On the phone

When running the business from home, consider who will be picking up the phone! It's cheap and sometimes free to get an 0845 local rate number or an 0870 national rate number for your business. This will hide where you're based and divert your calls to wherever you specify. But beware: sometimes having such a number – especially with national rates – might put customers off ringing you.

If you use a landline number it's best to have a separate line for your home and your business. These days you don't need to invest in an actual second line. You can use a VoIP (voice over internet protocol) phone, which uses a broadband internet connection to make and receive calls, something we looked at earlier.

- Skype | www.skype.com

Another idea is to get some help from a call-handling service. They will answer your calls with your company name, text urgent messages to you and email the others, giving you a big business feel for about £50 per month. Services on offer include:

- Moneypenny | www.moneypenny.co.uk
- Regus | www.regus.co.uk
- MyRuby | www.myruby.co.uk
- Answer | www.answer.co.uk

You might consider a 'follow-me number' to ensure you're available when you need to be and able to deliver the right impression to clients. A follow-me number involves choosing a number and directing calls from it to your landline or mobile. The beauty of choosing a number is that you have the option to select either a freephone or a geographical number so, say you'd like to have a Manchester area code, simply buy a number starting with 0161. The same goes for hundreds of other locations.

Offer virtual phone numbers where the caller pays a local rate, regardless of where you are, through Vonage (www.vonage.co.uk) or direct calls to you from a chosen number using internet technology and a virtual receptionist at eReceptionist (www.ereceptionist.co.uk).

In person

You are about to attend your first networking event or trade show and want to create a good first impression. With an attractive business card in hand, directing prospective customers to a good-looking online presence, all you have to do is follow the rules of effective networking!

The art of networking

- Wear your name tag (if you have one) on your right side. It's easy to catch sight of when you are shaking hands.

- Deliver a nice firm handshake and make eye contact.

- Say your name clearly and, in under ten seconds, tell the other person who you are and what you do.

- Listen carefully. Ask the other person plenty of questions about their line of business, their hobbies, etc.

- Be positive and energetic.

- Swap business cards.

- Send a thank-you email after the event, confirming any actions you and they have promised.

- Keep in regular and meaningful contact.

See Chapter 12 for information on how to host your own event or attend a trade show to promote your business.

A MEMORABLE EXCHANGE: Richard Moross, founder of moo.com, says: "The point of having a business card is to make a connection, create a relationship and leave something with the recipient that reminds them of you. Have cards that tell a story. Use that card as a sales tool, for sure, but also show appreciation by having cards relating to your customer." Richard achieves this by having images on his cards showing places he's visited and meals he's eaten. With 70% of moo.com's business being outside the UK, Richard travels a lot and the cards act as the ice-breaker in meetings as he tells the story behind the pictures.

11. MAKE SALES

With a professional image established, you are ready to start making sales. This chapter will help you achieve that first sale, plus provide tips on how to make money from your website or blog.

1. Make a list (check it twice)

Draw on your existing resources, grab your address book and select the friends, family, colleagues and acquaintances you think might be interested in your product or service. Add to the list with details of local people and businesses, too.

2. Pitch up

Contact the people on your list and announce your new business venture. Consider this an opportunity to make your pitch, but don't be too pushy. Remember to address each recipient personally. No one likes a group email!

3. Follow up

Follow up in a few days time, either with another email or, better still, a phone call. Take some soundings as to the success of your pitch and react accordingly. If the potential customer or client sounds keen, go for it! Arrange to meet him or her to show your product or explain more about your service.

4. Meet up

Arrange a time and place to meet that's convenient for your potential customer or client. Be professional, but also likeable. These are equally important characteristics when making a sale.

If the customer agrees the deal, bring the meeting to a fairly speedy end. Your job is done – for now. It's time to head home and deliver on the promise you made with your first customer.

5. Make some noise

Once you've made your first sale – shout about it! If your new customer or client agrees, include them in a press release or write about them on your website or blog, so other potential customers or clients can see that you're well and truly in business!

SALES ARE FLYING HIGH: Have promotional flyers made to take to events or deliver through doors. Increase chances of turning flyers into firm sales by:

- having a design that is memorable, possibly quirky and, ideally, that your potential customers will want to keep on their desk/in their bag/atop the kitchen shelf

- making the offer clear and confirming the benefits of buying

- including a call to action, i.e. a way in which the interested customer can contact you.

Warm up for a cold call

*Sales and marketing pro Jackie Wade (*www.winningsales.co.uk*) offers tips on how to make winning calls to customers . . .*

"**Ready:** Preparation and focus is key. Start with a call list and clear objectives; which business or household and who specifically are you calling (decision maker)? Are you clear on your message? What benefits do you offer?

"**Steady:** Feel confident, think positive. What's the worst thing that can happen? They may say no... so what! Not everyone out there will want you, but someone will! Tone is more important than words so feel and sound confident and positive.

"**Go:** Be natural, be you. Have a good opening 'hook' to grab attention – something interesting, new or different and make it relevant to the person you're calling. Avoid rambling – focus on a two-way conversation, not a fixed script. Develop a list of open questions which will allow you to engage with the person at the other end of the line, e.g. what do you currently do, how does it work, what might you like to improve? Listen for opportunities. Engage!

"**Grow:** Agree action and follow up promptly or agree a call back, if no interest for now. A NO today may be a YES tomorrow; tenacity counts. Things change.

"Remember, smile and then dial. Your aim is to spread the word about you and your business."

Selling into physical stores

Maybe you've started by selling products direct to customers at shows and fairs, but what about making sales via local shops?

Before you approach any shops, make a list of appropriate places where you think your product could work well. For example, does your town have gift shops or an art gallery, are there lots of boutiques that stock a range of different items? Think outside the box. Could your local coffee shop stock some of your items?

Five top tips for market placement

Laura Rigney is the author of *Pitching Products for Small Business* and offers five top tips for pitching your product effectively:

1. Be confident with pricing

"Selling in wholesale is a whole new ballpark as far as pricing is concerned. Make your product attractive to buyers with your pricing. A great way to show you're trying to help retailers is to setup a structured pricing system, i.e. 100 units or less £xx per unit, 101-500 units £xx per unit and 501 units or more £xx per unit. This system could also encourage shops and buyers to place larger orders.

2. Understand your product inside out

"This means technical data as well as knowing why someone would buy it. When you get a meeting with a buyer or approach a shop owner, talk with confidence about where the product is made, by who, and using what kind of materials. Remember there is pressure on large retailers to "go green", so the more you can offer that as a potential supplier the more attractive you will be.

3. Be prepared

"If a buyer places an order, how quickly will you have manufacturing, distribution and storage in place? Buyers won't expect a new small business to have a giant factory sitting waiting for someone to press the 'go' button but they will want a realistic estimate of how long it will be until your product is in their warehouses/on the shop shelf. Once you have given your timings, stick to them. Even if this means exaggerating the time it will take for them to be delivered. Better to be early rather than late!

4. Pitch perfect

"If you're pitching in person, make it informative, exciting and interesting and where possible have evidence of past sales and customer satisfaction. You need to know your figures without having to look through paperwork and be prepared to haggle a little on prices. If someone likes your product enough and you have sold it well enough they will buy it, even if it's a few pennies more than they would like to pay. In the other direction, sometimes it may be worth offering a larger than normal discount as a trial for a first order.

5. Stay listed

"When a company takes on your product it's called being listed. Once you are listed the work is just beginning! It is now time to stay listed for as long as possible and the way to do this is through marketing and PR. The more you promote your product and the shops/galleries/boutiques that are selling them, the more they will be bought by consumers thus encouraging buyers to place more orders with you!"

PITCH POTENTIAL: Visit the Enterprise Nation pledge site to view the big businesses opening up their supply chains to small ones – i.e. ideal pitch opportunities for you! **www.greatbusinessexchange.co.uk**

Dean Tempest knows about getting stocked in stores; this is exactly what he's achieved for the now popular family game, Linkee . . .

CASE STUDY

NAME: Dean Tempest | BUSINESS: Linkee

Dean Tempest didn't come up with the original idea for "shouty-outy quiz game" Linkee. He says it's more like he ran into it by being in the right place, at the right time.

'I wasn't enjoying my job working at a London advertising agency so went looking for something a bit more interesting to get stuck in to within the agency and heard about this new game people were playing in our creative department. I found the lads who had created it and asked if I could get involved."

The game had been invented and played in various guises a good five years before Dean came along. What eventually became Linkee was an idea dreamt up by a copywriter called Tris and one half of an advertising creative team.

"A keen game fan, Tris created Linkee one Christmas for his family to play. Working with Ben, an art director, and Tris's creative partner, they got to work at honing the idea. Then I came along and helped build the case for Linkee as a business.

"We could all see the potential in what was essentially a handmade box of cards that had sat in an office drawer for five years but we didn't know how well people would take to it.

"Whilst juggling our existing jobs we spent a good six months exploring the opportunity, visiting trade shows and trying to find out as much as we could about the industry from research papers and people within the industry. We also held Linkee quiz nights to properly test the product. With no mortgage or kids I was the best out of the three of us to take the plunge and leave my job, so I did."

Dean would speak about the product to anybody who would listen.

"It's amazing how many people would say, 'Oh, I know a bloke who's done this, or worked here, give them a call.' I would call them no matter how tenuous the link. Turned out my granddad played golf with somebody who worked at Waddingtons back in the day; he helped with some great industry insights. Our printer recommended a client of his called, Peter Seagar, now a great friend of Linkee. Peter had got some very successful games including, Where is Moldova, stocked in John Lewis and lots of other larger retailers. He helped us massively. This went on and on. The key person, though, was our chairman, who I met in the advertising industry. I was 24 when I set up Linkee and knew I wanted somebody with experience to help us along the way; and he was only too willing."

Even at the age of 24, Dean knew he wanted to get the product stocked in high street stores. But how to go about it?

"Finding the contacts isn't difficult – you often just need to pick up the phone. It's getting them to take an interest in what you are doing that is hard. We found it wasn't just a case of having a good product: buyers want to see examples of where it has sold already, and know how you are going to drive people to buy it if they stock it.

"In our first Christmas (the key trading period) we had three shops selling Linkee. These were smaller regional department stores that were slightly easier to access, and we had sold Linkee to them at cost price. We couldn't afford to print enough to be able to make a margin selling through retail at that point. But that didn't matter; it was about building the case study for the trade shows in January. We did everything we could to make sure Linkee sold well in those stores, using demoing, point of sale and local PR. The Daniel Department Store in Windsor was our key location, and at one point there we were outselling Trivial Pursuit. This was the data we needed.

"We've always known that, when people play Linkee, they seem to get it and like it. So we spent all that we had left and took small stands at three trade shows where we knew the buyers would be. We shared a space at one show with Peter Seagar, who I mentioned earlier. He kindly helped with some introductions but that didn't stop us from having to run after the John Lewis buyer to get them to have a play. This was Tris's 20 seconds of courage that had a massive ripple effect on the business. Once we got stocked in John Lewis, people began to take us more seriously."

Selling in a pop-up shop also helped.

"The pop-up shop was a great education in how to merchandise and sell our product directly. As a small business, with literally no retail presence, it helped us have some point of reference for sales data. It was a necessary education and what we learned helped in early conversations with larger buyers."

What also helped is that a number of the buyers would have seen Dean and Linkee on *Dragons' Den*!

"Appearing on the show was an invaluable exercise. We were the 12-minute feature edit that night. Overnight over three million people had heard of Linkee, essentially a business being run out of the corner of the lounge in my shared rented flat. The first marketing service we ever spent money on was PR and this really helped us to make the most of the exposure. But the exposure would have meant nothing if retailers couldn't access the product, so most importantly we formed a distribution agreement with John Adams, a leading toy and game company in the UK, who sold into every major retailer in the country.

"We did need funds but not loads at the very beginning. I didn't take a salary, we didn't have an office, we just needed enough for small print runs. We started with £20,000 that we all contributed from our own savings. We did look at VCs, and of course *Dragons' Den*, but as such a young company with no big trading record we knew we'd have to give away more than we were probably comfortable with, which was true with *Dragons' Den*. So instead we renegotiated terms with our supplier and borrowed another £20,000. This was the best thing we did: now all our debts are paid off and we own all of our company."

With the company in their hands and all three founders now full time, this business is continuing to go places.

"The plan now is to grow by geography and range. We have moved towards a licensing model, so we let experienced games companies in the UK and abroad do what they do best: manufacture and distribute, and leave us doing what we do best: marketing, product development and brand building. We've also just completed a new version of Linkee for the UK which will be launched in March 2014 with our UK licensing partner, John Adams, and plan to launch Dinkee Linkee, our children's version, whilst pushing our app forward."

Linkee has gone from an office drawer to the shelves of high street stores, and in so doing this business shows what's possible when you combine determination, hard work and the courage to ask people for help.

● **www.playlinkee.com** | @playlinkee

TOP TIP: "Surround yourself with people you like, who are enthusiastic about what you are doing and know more than you do. This applies to everybody: suppliers, distributors, retailers and even competitors. It worked for us!"

Lucy Woodhouse and business partner Meriel successfully pitched their frozen-yoghurt lollies to Sainsbury's as part of StartUp Britain's PitchUp competition. As a result, their lollies will launch exclusively with Sainsbury's in May 2014. Lucy says the secret to their success was:

- "a genuinely new product"
- "identifying our target audience"
- "really knowing the market"
- "being very aware of food trends and incorporating them into the products so we were ahead of the game, newsworthy and desirable"
- "a passionate pitch that didn't use Powerpoint".

PopUps

Want to hone retail skills, meet customers face to face and make sales? Why not try a high street PopUp and test new markets in the flesh?

PopUp Britain (www.popupbritain.co.uk) was created to give new British brands an opportunity to get onto the high street and fill empty shops with small business activity. A first PopUp store opened in Richmond in July 2012 and, 12 shops later, the project has welcomed hundreds of start-ups and small businesses that trade in the shop for a week or fortnight before moving on to allow new businesses to move in.

The PopUp tenants are all online businesses that don't normally have the budget to take on a shop single-handedly and full time. PopUp Britain brings tenants together to share the cost and workload.

The project has delivered a national 'PopUp Lease' (courtesy of Nick Darby at Denton's) which makes contractual arrangements with landlords a whole lot simpler. The PopUp scene in the UK is flourishing with two platforms on the market that enable small businesses to easily find and book retail and PopUp space. They are We Are PopUp www.wearepopup.com and Appear Here www.appearhere.co.uk .

The art of the pop

Here's how to ensure your PopUp experience is a profitable one.

- **P**lace – choose a shop in a location that suits your products and is populated with people who represent your target market.

- **O**ffer – ahead of moving into the shop, prepare sufficient stock at a price that's right for the particular area. Present the produce in a way that will attract customers' attention. Consider your own presentation and body language when approaching and dealing with customers.

- **P**romote – now you're in the shop, tell people you're there! Promote your presence to existing customers through social media. To attract new trade, consider partnerships with neighbouring retailers, flyers in the train station, releases to the local press and PopUp parties, lock-ins, cook-offs and fashion shows, to deliver a retail experience that customers will never forget!

Get the POP right and you'll see sales and profile on the UP!

For Eleanor Stuart, taking part in a PopUp shop was her most effective marketing exercise to date . . .

CASE STUDY

NAME: Eleanor Stuart | BUSINESS: Eleanor Stuart

Before starting her own business, illustrator and designer (and recent graduate) Eleanor Stuart spent a year working for an events company in London.

"It was whilst working with this company that an opportunity came up to design *Alice in Wonderland* plates for a themed event. Having always loved design and illustration, I jumped at the chance. After creating those first plates and seeing such a positive reaction to them, I realised I could have the first few products of a business."

Eleanor launched her own illustration and design business in May 2013 with strong support from the creative community.

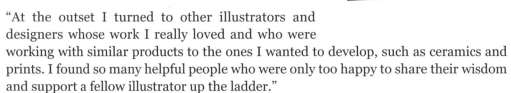

"At the outset I turned to other illustrators and designers whose work I really loved and who were working with similar products to the ones I wanted to develop, such as ceramics and prints. I found so many helpful people who were only too happy to share their wisdom and support a fellow illustrator up the ladder."

"When it comes to inspiration for my designs, I find this by being out and about – especially in London. I'm most inspired by other people's work, so I can often be found in galleries or treading the boards of Liberty. I try to create work with a sense of humour and friends and family are my testbed. If a new piece makes them smile, I know I've got it right."

Eleanor was keen to keep production in Britain as she felt it would be more practical than overseas manufacturing and wanted the stamp of quality associated with the 'Made in Britain' tag.

"When I was looking for a pottery to produce my fine bone china plates, there was nowhere else to turn other than the heart of the British pottery industry, Stoke-on-Trent. This is where I found a fantastic pottery to work with who have become integral to the quality of my ceramic pieces.

"After much time, research and samples, I was also able to find suppliers from across the UK, from Kent to Norfolk, and it's been wonderful working with companies who have a real dedication to creating a quality product."

The business started out selling online but having retail stockists was always the big dream for Eleanor.

"Getting my work into the real world was a big step that was made possible with the help of PopUp Britain, who provided the amazing opportunity to be part of a pop-up shop in Piccadilly Circus. The experience of having my work on sale in a physical space and the success I enjoyed whilst selling in the shop showed me the potential of having my work stocked in other shops. I even secured my first stockist, the British Library, whilst in the PopUp!

"That first pop-up shop (which I went on to do again in time for Christmas) was the most effective marketing exercise for my business. It gave me an incredible opportunity to not only showcase my work for the first time, but to receive feedback from customers and meet some very interesting people. Being in Piccadilly Circus meant being able to mingle with buyers from places such as Fortnum & Mason and Waterstones, which were on the same street, so it was an exercise in marketing and great for networking with buyers and other businesses in the shop. In a word, it was brilliant!"

After the pop-up, Eleanor went on to secure one of her dream stockists: designer department store, Liberty, in London.

"To be approached by one of the top shops on my list so soon after launching my business was a bit of a 'pinch me I'm day-dreaming' moment but very exciting at the same time."

This young business owner continues to have plenty of plans in the pipeline, with upcoming trade shows and launching two new collections.

"I find that reminding myself on a daily basis of the goals I want to achieve helps me outline the steps to take each day to get me closer to achieving those goals. It's also important to take stock of what you have achieved. Sometimes setting off into the world of starting your own business can feel overwhelming when you have your head buried in Excel sheets and emails, so standing back and giving yourself a little thumbs up now and again can motivate you to keep going."

For all she has achieved in such a short space of time, it's a big thumbs up for Eleanor from here.

- **www.eleanorstuart.com** | @Eleanor_Stuart

TOP TIP: "Talk to people! There are people who have done it before and who are probably willing to offer advice and help. In the beginning, identifying people whose work I admired and contacting them with my very long list of questions really helped settle my nerves about starting a business."

For Alexandra van Berckel, a pop-up shop has led to plans for a permanent retail space, showing that pop-ups truly are a route to testing the market before committing to a long lease and serious investment . . .

CASE STUDY

NAME: Alexandra van Berckel | BUSINESS: Pinucci

Sketching since she attended her first art class at school, Alexandra van Berckel began her career as an architect before moving into design, finally leading to the creation of her young footwear business, Pinucci.

"Starting Pinucci was a natural evolution for me. Designing shoes allows me to combine my love of fashion with my passion for design. My mother owned a boutique so I think something in my background has played a part in the creation of Pinucci too."

Pinucci shoes are designed in Alexandra's London studio and handcrafted in Spanish and Italian artisan workshops that have been in the same families for generations.

"When deciding on which workshops we would partner with, this human element was very important. Keeping our carbon footprint low and producing ethically and sustainably within Europe is as important to us as producing shoes that are high quality."

The shoes are sold online and have been sold via PopUp Britain shops in prime London locations including Piccadilly, Kings Road and Victoria.

"Every store is compellingly curated by the PopUp Britain team and each one offers a diverse merchandise mix in which customers can browse and discover unique products and experience brands selected from all over Britain.

"Each week there are usually between six and ten brands featured, depending on the size of the store. What made the difference for us was the fact that the PopUp Britain team not only creates the pop-up event, but also provides essential behind-the-scenes support such as PR, legal help, card payment facilities and insurance. Each brand is also paired with a visual merchandising expert who helps set up products, making them look stunning, so all the brands have to do is focus on introducing the brand to customers."

Alexandra benefited not only from selling shoes to customers but also in meeting fellow traders.

"Part of the ethos of PopUp Britain is that we all sell each other's products as well as our own and in every store all the brands are encouraged to work together as a collaborative effort within the shared retail space – it is very much like how a department store works – and as we know, successful retail businesses depend on different teams working well with each other.

"By meeting and building a rapport with other start-up entrepreneurs from a range of business and cultural backgrounds we have increased our network and many collaborations have developed."

The company used the opportunity of popping up in Piccadilly to introduce key pieces from their spring/summer 2014 collection, which had been shown in Milan at a trade show but not yet shown to the public.

"Being in Piccadilly was unique; where else can you get to speak with a buyer from Fortnum & Mason (who we're delighted to say loved our men's shoes) and meet DTZ, the corporate real estate and facilities management specialists, who suggested we were a great brand for Westfield – all on the same day? As a direct result from being in the PopUp Piccadilly store we are in discussions with a bespoke tailors and have been approached by a UK-wide menswear label looking to stock some of our new season's men's collection.

"For Pinucci, discovering our customers and being discovered by customers is always a delight. With British and international customers coming in the shop across the week we were able to gauge which models (and colours) will be most popular because of the instant customer reaction and feedback. It's very exciting for us that we have a growing waiting list with lots of pre-orders for our new spring/summer 2014 collection and we're delighted that our website is seeing a rise in unique visitors. We handed out more than 400 cards, lookbooks and postcards and it seems that people did then make the time to look us up."

Back in the studio, Pinucci continues to work on expansion plans including a partnership with STK in The Strand to showcase during London Collections, becoming a member of the British Footwear Association and, critically, opening its first retail unit.

'The vision is to develop and evolve men and women's collections whilst keeping true to our philosophy of creating footwear that is heritage inspired but contemporary in design, sustainably made in our Artisanal workshops.'

Expect to see this up and coming brand on the High Street soon!

- **www.pinucci.com** | @frompinucci

TOP TIP: "Be passionate and don't be afraid to fail and start again, not every idea leaves the drawing board."

Going global

Of the 18 businesses profiled in this kit, 70% are trading overseas; making sales via the platform sites or selling directly into new markets through local contacts and/or assistance from UK Trade & Investment.

To discover more about the specifics of international trade and how to go global in five basic steps, download a free eBook (tinyurl.com/goglobalguide) which offers all you need to know on topics from customs documentation to website translation and perfecting the art of cultural etiquette.

- Go Global on Enterprise Nation | **tinyurl.com/goglobalEN**
- DHL blog | **www.dhlguide.co.uk/blog**
- UK Trade & Investment | **www.ukti.gov.uk**
- Alibaba | **www.alibaba.com**

In her first year of trading Sally Guyer sold more of her product overseas than in the UK. And promotion was all through social media . . .

CASE STUDY

NAME: Sally Guyer | BUSINESS: Cambridge Raincoat Company

Sally Guyer has a part-time job teaching English to international students. The rest of the time she runs her business, Cambridge Raincoat Company, designing and selling coats.

The initial idea was a stylish solution for cyclists – beautifully designed fashion items that would be breathable, wind-proof, washable, water resistant and durable. But Sally saw items from both her men and women's range become all-year-round fashionable pieces.

"Being made in Britain is still synonymous with quality and being classy. My first sale was to the USA, thanks to the reach of the internet. In the first year of trading I sold more overseas than I did in the UK. The coats weigh less than a kilo and I post them myself. Promotion has largely been through Twitter and Facebook. I also won £15,000-worth of local advertising in January 2012 which has helped a lot with local promotion, as you can imagine!"

Sally plans to continue with the international push and has been approached by potential agents in Germany and China who only deal with British-made goods. Her ultimate ambition is to have the business turning over sufficient income so that she can give up the part-time job and focus full time on what is already a global business!

- www.cambridgeraincoats.co.uk | @cantala59

Make money from your website

As traffic to your blog increases, so does your chance of generating income. Make a profit from your posts with this top-ten list of options.

1. Display advertising

Offer advertising on your site. The more niche your audience, the more likely you are to attract advertisers.

The information you'll need to provide includes:

- number of unique visitors
- number of impressions
- average duration of visit
- visitor demographics.

Write a basic rate card (see a few pages' time), add it to your site and send it to corporate marketing departments and media-buying agencies.

2. Google AdSense

This tool from Google does the work for you by placing relevant ads on your site and earning you money when people click on them. You can customise the appearance of the ads so they sit well with the style of your site.

- www.google.co.uk/adsense

3. Text Link Ads

These ads offer direct click-throughs from text on your site. You submit your site to Text Link Ads and then upload the ad code provided. It's your choice whether you approve or deny the supplied ads. Once that's done, you start making money as visitors click on the ads. Try this and Skimlinks, which converts words on your site to affiliate links so that you earn from those, too.

- www.text-link-ads.com
- www.skimlinks.com

4. Sponsored conversations

Get paid for posts (and now tweets) with services like IZEA that match bloggers with advertisers. Some doubt the ethical stance of paying a blogger to write something about a product but there's no doubt that it's a money maker.

- www.izea.com

5. Affiliate schemes

Sign up to affiliate schemes like the Amazon Associates Programme, where you can earn up to 10% in referrals by advertising Amazon products. The programme works by driving traffic to Amazon.co.uk through specially formatted links. You earn referral fees on sales generated through those links. Monthly cheques are sent to you from Amazon and it's easy and free to join.

- affiliate-program.amazon.co.uk

6. Sponsored features

This could include a host of options. Approach advertisers with suggestions of a sponsored eBook, e-news, podcast, webchat, poll or survey. These applications can be added to your site at a low cost yet generate good revenue.

For:

- eBook creation, try www.blurb.com
- a survey or poll feature, try www.surveymonkey.com
- email marketing, try www.mailchimp.com

7. Expert help

Offer your expertise and charge people to log on and watch or listen. This could be made available through teleclasses where you invite customers and contacts onto a call where you offer your expertise on a one-to-many basis, or an email training course using email programs such as Mailchimp (www.mailchimp.com) or Constant Contact (www.constantcontact.co.uk), or deliver a presentation to potentially thousands of paying customers via www.gotowebinar.co.uk.

8. Deals with suppliers

Do deals with suppliers. Hosting a travel blog? Agree a percentage each time a booking is made via your site. Hosting a wedding blog? Create a directory of wedding suppliers such as venues, photographers, dressmakers and caterers with an enhanced listing for those who pay.

9. Turn a blog into a book

Follow the lead of Alex Johnson who turned his Shedworking blog (**www.shedworking.co.uk**) into a book – and then a second book – which are now selling across the UK and overseas, acting as an effective marketing tool for the site!

10. Please donate

If you'd rather just ask for a small donation from your visitors, this is possible too via a donate feature from PayPal. Add a PayPal donate button to your site: **bit.ly/ikf832**

* * *

Maybe you've decided to start selling products through your site. But if you only carry content, you'll need to add an e-commerce feature to make sales.

> **JUST-IN-TIME PAYMENT:** Add a PayPal payment button to your site and you'll be able to accept payment from all major credit and debit cards, as well as bank accounts around the world. You can set it up in less than 15 minutes.

Add an e-commerce plug-in

Want to open your site up to sales? Do so by plugging in an e-commerce tool such as:

- WordPress e-Commerce shopping cart – "suitable for selling your products, services, or fees online": **bit.ly/fEgQHo**
- PayPal Shortcodes – insert PayPal buttons in your posts or pages using a Shortcode: **bit.ly/KGNE5f**
- View a complete list of WordPress e-commerce plugins: **bit.ly/eTEkwZ**

Add a shopping cart to your site

Make it easy for your visitors to click and buy. Check out these shopping cart providers:

- GroovyCart | www.groovycart.co.uk
- RomanCart | www.romancart.com
- CubeCart | www.cubecart.com
- Zen Cart | www.zen-cart.com
- ekmPowershop | www.ekmpowershop.com
- osCommerce | www.oscommerce.com

Research the product that suits you best, taking into account hosting provision, back-end admin, and built-in search engine optimisation.

SHOW ME YOUR RATES! The purpose of a media rate card is to show potential advertisers what your site can deliver to them in terms of traffic and sales. To do this, include some key points:

- **A brief description of the site:** What it does and for whom.

- **Visitor demographics:** Do you have data on the age of your visitors, their home region, gender, etc? If so, include it, as it helps build a picture of your audience.

- **Site traffic:** What are your unique visitor numbers and length of time spent on the site? Make a note if the figures are increasing.

- **Costings:** Do you have a cost-per-click (CPC) or cost-per-impression (CPM) rate? If so, include it here, along with the price of other sponsorship options. Offer a menu but leave some flexibility, with 'costed on a project basis' for sponsor features that would benefit from a more tailored proposal.

- **Screen shots:** Showing how and where adverts or sponsored features appear on the site.

- **Media activity:** Note where you've recently been covered in the media, online and off, so that potential sponsors can see how and where you're promoting the site.

- **Testimonials:** Positive comments from existing sponsors gives you credibility and gives confidence to the next potential sponsor.

- **Team details:** Who are the faces behind the site and what are their credentials? In other words, your background career and activities, etc.

Round this off with your contact details so that interested potential sponsors can get in touch and place an order!

12. MAKE SOME NOISE!

Sales are coming in, customers are happy and you want to tell the world about you and your new business. Profile brings new customers and new sales. Get yourself known in the press and online by making friends with the media, hosting events, entering awards and embracing social media.

Here's what to do.

Plot the script

Imagine yourself as the star of your own Hollywood movie. Are you an action hero, battling against the odds (think James Dyson) or a brand leading lady (think Mary Portas)? Plot the action and write the script. It will help you define your message to the media.

Find the right contacts

Research the journalists you think are interested in your field. Note their email addresses from the bottom of their articles, follow them on Twitter, get to know them and send them exclusive stories about you and your business.

LINK REQUEST: If you're being featured online ask the journalist if they can include a live link to your site. That way, readers can be on your site with one click.

Write a release

Writing a press release costs nothing but your time, yet it can generate thousands of pounds' worth of publicity. If you're emailing a press release to journalists, write the text in the body of the email and include it in an attachment, too.

Your press release should have an attention-grabbing headline, the main facts in the first sentence, and evidence and quotes from as high-profile people and companies as possible in the main body of the text. Include great quality images wherever you can to lift the piece and put a face to the brand.

You could also use a press-release distribution service to secure wider exposure. My personal favourite is ResponseSource (**www.responsesource.com**) but there's also PR Newswire (**www.prnewswire.co.uk**) and PRWeb (**www.prweb.com**).

If you don't get a response, follow up!

AN IMAGE SPEAKS LOUDER THAN WORDS: When a picture speaks a thousand words you can afford to talk less! Consider hiring a professional photographer to take pictures of you and your work. Maybe you can do this as a barter deal? Or pick up your own digital camera and do it yourself. Consider approaching a local college to suggest a photography student takes your images in exchange for including the end result in their portfolio. A journalist is much more likely to cover your story if you have great imagery to go with it. Use the images on your website and in promotion materials, and let your business speak for itself.

Example press release

1. Attention-grabbing headline, followed by bulletpoint summary of whole story

2. The first line is punchy and explains the what, who, why and where of the headline

3. Back up the headline and intro with more detail – facts and figures if you have them

4. Include a quote from you (or your business partner, if relevant)

5. Can you include a quote from someone else? A happy customer, industry expert or celebrity?

6. End with a call to action. Where can people go to find out more/how to download the report/which site to visit to claim a free gift, etc.?

7. Include 'Notes to Editors', with brief details on you and your company

8. Remember to include contact details – your email address and telephone number

9. Attach a relevant and interesting image

1.

GROWTH VOUCHER MARKETPLACE GOES TO SMALL BUSINESS NETWORK

- **Small business network wins competitive pitch to deliver Growth Vouchers**
- **£30m of vouchers for small business to spend on accredited business advice**
- **Enterprise Nation's winning proposal gathers private sector funding to build, oversee and administer voucher scheme advice**

2.

A small business network has announced it has been selected to deliver the Government's £30m Growth Voucher marketplace. Enterprise Nation won the competitive pitch with its proposal to use only private sector funding to build, market and administer the vouchers marketplace, which will connect small businesses with accredited business experts.

3.

The single platform will offer strategic advisers in finance, marketing, PR, general business and planning with the expertise to help small businesses grow. The vouchers will provide a Government-funded contribution towards the cost of advice for selected businesses.

The typical value allocated to a small business will be £2,000.

4.

Emma Jones MBE, founder of Enterprise Nation and co-founder of national enterprise campaign StartUp Britain, said: "This is an exciting initiative which could help accelerate the growth of thousands of small businesses at a critical stage of development – helping them to build long-term sustainability.

"At the moment, access to business advice is sporadic and unregulated with no means available to understand the outcomes.

"By bringing together accredited business advisers with the entrepreneurs that want to access good advice, we think the marketplace has the potential to deliver a significant boost to economic growth."

5.

In his report Growing Your Business 2013, the Prime Minister's Enterprise Adviser Lord Young said firms who "seek and engage external business advice are more likely to grow. But much more needs to be done to encourage firms to invest in their capability."

The Growth Vouchers scheme will be launched early next year and vouchers will be available until March 2015. The delivery of the vouchers will be part of a random-testing exercise to help the Government gain a better understanding of the effect of business advice on growth and the wider economic implications of Government intervention.

Enterprise Nation has a membership of over 75,000 small and start-up businesses. It delivers a comprehensive package of advice for entrepreneurs including tips and advice on starting and growing a business, expert events, and well-attended start-up courses across the UK.

The platform is funded by private sector brands technology specialist Toshiba, co-working expert Regus, cloud provider Citrix, telecoms brand Vodafone, cloud-based accounts and payroll software provider Sage One, energy provider, EDF Energy and online insurance company, Simply Business, which are showing their support for business by backing the initiative.

The scheme comes in the context of record numbers of start-up businesses across the UK, with more than half a million new registered companies expected by the end of 2013 for the first time.

9.

6.

To register interest in the Marketplace, please visit **www.enterprisenation.com/marketplace**

7.

ABOUT ENTERPRISE NATION: Enterprise Nation is a small business network with more than 75,000 members. Its aim is to help people turn their good ideas into great businesses – through expert advice, events, networking and inspiring books. Enterprise Nation was founded in 2005 by Emma Jones MBE also co-founder of StartUp Britain.

For media enquiries, please contact Lizzie Slee (01234) 567 890 liz@enterprisenation.com

8.

Tweet, Tweet

Follow media channels, journalists and personalities on Twitter so you're the first to pick up the news and media requests. View this post to start following the UK's top 45 small business journalists: www.enterprisenation.com/blog/posts/45-small-business-journalists-to-follow-on-twitter

FREE PR CONSULTATION: Join Enterprise Nation and benefit from a free PR consultation with media pro, Liz Slee, who works tirelessly to place small businesses all across the press: **www.enterprisenation.com/join**

KICK-STARTING WITH PR

Greg Simpson, founder and director of Press for Attention PR (**www.pressforattention.com**) gives his top 12 tips for building a successful PR campaign:

1. HAVE A 'CUNNING PLAN'

"Too many people rush into PR and marketing campaigns with no real plan. You need to consider:

"What are the goals of the campaign?

"How do you want to come across in terms of tone?

"Key messages – what do you want to get across?

2. CONSIDER HOW OTHER COMPANIES GET THEIR MESSAGES ACROSS

"What tactics can you use? PR stunts, press releases, controversy, photo opportunities, comment/opinion pieces, debates, flash mobs, press trips, celebrity endorsements, competitions. There are so many ways to get noticed. Blend them to your requirements and skills.

3. RESEARCH YOUR CUSTOMER/AUDIENCE

"There is little point getting a full article page in *Dog Grooming Monthly* if you sell organic ice cream to boutique hotels! Find out who your ideal customer is and research what they read, listen to and watch. Then, really take the time to read these publications and get to know what sort of stories they publish.

4. FIND THE NEWS HOOK

"Be honest, is your story really news? Examples include: new products, new staff, new promotions, new premises, anniversaries, company expansion, financial milestones and charity efforts.

"You can also provide topical comment on a newsworthy subject. Keep an eye out for issues that affect your business or your customers. This takes practice and you need to establish credibility in your subject area first. Consider starting a blog that provides regular, lively and informed comment in your area of expertise to build your profile. I use WordPress (**www.wordpress.org**), which is free.

5. GOT A STORY?

"Got a story? Great! Now you need a simple press release for a journalist to refer to. People worry that their efforts don't sound flashy enough to warrant attention. But you aren't aiming for a Booker Prize. You're aiming for coherent and interesting *news*.

"Use 'who, what, when, how and why?' as a framework and imagine yourself as the journalist. Is this definitely of interest to their readers? Is it simple enough to understand? Does it stand up on its own?

"I would stick to a maximum of 300 words and keep the press release focused on the news angle.

6. HIT THEM BETWEEN THE EYES

"Journalists get hundreds of press releases every day. Ensure that the headline and first paragraph sum up the entire story in a nutshell. Ideally, your press release should still make sense even if an editor dropped two or three paragraphs.

"I call the journalist beforehand to outline my story. This helps iron out any creases and demonstrates that you are trying to work with them and their audience.

7. DON'T BE TEMPTED TO START HASSLING

"I very rarely 'chase' a journalist once I have sent a press release. If it is good enough, they will use it. Hassling will not push it to the top of the pile and may see it heading towards the recycle bin. Be patient and able to help if the journalist does come back and don't go on holiday the day after you have sent a story out!

8. THINK IN PICTURES

"Consider what makes you read a story when you flick through a newspaper. Headlines play their part but the impact of an interesting picture is greater still. People 'sell' stories, so ensure that anyone in your shot is clearly visible and captioned. Try to show the impact of the news – product shots are okay, but a product in the hands of a customer is better."

9. BUILD A RELATIONSHIP

"PR is not a 'them v us' war with journalists. It's a working relationship, where both parties stand to gain. They get news/insight and you get free publicity in exchange for a fresh take on things or for your role in illustrating the impact of an issue.

10. MEASURE AND EVALUATE

"How do you know if your gym regime and new diet is working? You get on the scales (peeking between your fingers). Are you getting through to the right journalists? How many stories are you sending out? How many are getting coverage? How much coverage do they get? Do your pictures and even your key messages get included? Are you being invited to comment on topical issues?

Enter awards

Enter awards and competitions and enjoy the press coverage that goes with it. Many award schemes are free to enter and are targeted at young start-up businesses. Writing the entry will help to clarify your goals and vision, and winning will bring profile and prizes. To find out about upcoming awards across the UK, follow Enterprise Nation as we blog and tweet about the best of them!

Here are some to get you started:

- Shell LiveWIRE Grand Ideas Awards (**www.shell-livewire.org/awards**) – up to four awards per month of £1,000 for anyone aged 16 to 30 and looking to get an idea off the ground.

- The Pitch (**www.thepitchuk.com**) – enter regional heats and pitch to experienced judges for a place in the national finals and a £50,000 prize. Takes place across the UK.

- *Country Living* Magazine Kitchen Table Talent Awards (**www.kitchen tabletalent.com**) – if you're working on a talent or skill from the kitchen table and know it can be turned into a business, this competition is for you. Prizes include office equipment and profile in the magazine, which can be very good for sales!

- Social Enterprise Awards (**www.socialenterprise.org.uk/events**) – celebrates social enterprises of all ages.

- Nectar Small Business Awards (**www.nectar.com/dynamic/smallbusiness**) – offers cash prizes and plenty of Nectar points!

- Startups Awards (**www.startups.co.uk/startups-awards**) – celebrating small businesses of all shapes and sizes.

- Smarta100 (**www.smarta.com/smarta100**) – an annual award to find Britain's brightest businesses with a grand prize of £10,000 in cash to the winner decided by popular vote.

- Rise To (**www.riseto.co.uk**) – an enterprise challenge developed by the Prelude Group (backed by The Supper Club and Red Bull) that attracts entries from teams of entrepreneurial students across the country, who each have to run a campaign championing a cause that's close to their hearts (previous winners have championed teachers, midwives and paramedics). The best teams and individuals are eligible for prizes and unique work experience shadowing successful entrepreneurs.

Jordan Bourke has seen at first-hand the benefits of entering awards . . .

CASE STUDY

NAME: Jordan Bourke | BUSINESS: The Guilt Free Gourmet

Even before he's officially started trading, Jordan Bourke is making waves and hitting the headlines. This young entrepreneur is a chef, food writer and food stylist for cookbooks, magazines and advertising shoots. He continues to work as a freelancer across these areas whilst starting a new business in food retail.

After success in securing a Shell LiveWIRE business award, Jordan went on to enter annual business competition, The Pitch.

'The Pitch has been incredibly helpful, mainly in terms of meeting people who are doing something similar to me but a few stages further along. The judges were extremely generous with their contacts and put me in touch with people at Gü Puds, Nairns Oatcakes and Ella's Kitchen. Their advice has been invaluable and saved me from making so many early mistakes.

"Since the Pitch my business has moved forward incredibly quickly as I learned through contacts made at the event that I can run my business in a different way by outsourcing production, packaging and distribution, so taking a large part of the pressure off me. As my business has not started trading yet I can't be sure of its success but participating in these competitions has made me a lot more confident."

Jordan is working on launching the brand and a business that will offer food products and ranges. A second cookbook is on its way and this guilt-free gourmet chef is set to continue writing for national publications to increase his own brand profile, which will in turn benefit the business. When it comes to raising a profile, he's got off to a strong start.

- www.jourdanbourke.com | @jordanbourk

TOP TIP: "Go to as many small business events as possible like StartUp Saturday, The Pitch, Shell LiveWIRE etc. The main reason I am where I am now is because I applied to these events and awards and met people who were able to advise me. At the end of the day, the more people you speak to about your business idea, the more feedback you receive, the more advice you get and ultimately the easier it is for you to refine your idea into the most commercially viable one."

Host an event

Invite the press to come and meet you. This doesn't have to be an expensive affair; the secret is partnering with others who could benefit from being in front of your audience. Approach a venue and ask if you can host at no cost, in exchange for the venue receiving profile. Do the same with caterers. Then give invited guests a reason to attend – have a theme, an interesting speaker, a launch announcement, something that will grab their attention and encourage them to attend.

Make use of free online services such as Eventbrite (**www.eventbrite.com**) or Meetup (**www.meetup.com**) to send out invites and receive RSVPs.

SUCCESSFUL EVENTS IN 5 STEPS

1. PLANNING = WINNING

BY EVENTBRITE

Plan your event so you don't forget anything important. When will the event be held? When do you need to find a venue? When will tickets go on sale? When will you find sponsors by? When do you need materials delivered?

2. TAKE IT ONLINE

Create an event page on Eventbrite so you can manage sign ups and communicate with attendees in one place. You can create custom URLs, promo codes and even different ticket types, such as an early bird rate.

3. PARTNER UP

Start-ups grow and thrive off the back of collaborations. Put your event idea to contacts in the same space or at a similar stage and make it a group effort.

4. GET PEOPLE TALKING

Be remarkable! Get creative and find a USP – an unusual venue, theme or format – so people remember your event. Once that's sorted, make the most of Eventbrite's social media integration to share your event... everywhere! And don't forget to create a Twitter hashtag so attendees can spread the word for you. #Bonus!

5. STAY IN TOUCH

The event doesn't end when guests leave. Write follow up emails, newsletters, tweets, or connect on LinkedIn, and thank guests for attending. Encourage them to stay in touch and add them to your email list so they are in the loop about your next great event!

Attend events

Be seen and heard by getting out and about – a lot!

There's a wealth of events for start-ups. Most are free or low cost and offer an opportunity to learn from experts, mix with peers, and find new customers and suppliers

Enterprise Nation hosts a whole range of events throughout the year designed to help you start and grow. We'd love to see you at some of them!

- StartUp Saturday – offering all you need to know to start a business in a day. Held throughout the year and across the UK.

- Member meet-ups – monthly get-togethers for members who want to meet peers, get support and find new trading partners

- Go & Grow Online – evening events covering the topics that matter most to growing businesses including social media, international payments, delivery and new market intelligence.

- Expert workshops – training courses of up to six weeks delivered by experts in the fields of tech, law, marketing, sales and accounts.

Full details for all of these can be found at the 'Events' section of www.enterprisenation.com.

In terms of events there's also . . .

- Global Entrepreneurship Week (November each year) | www.gew.org.uk
- NACUE events at universities and colleges | nacue.com
- StartUp Weekend: hosted in locations across the UK | www.startupweekend.org
- The Business StartUp Show | www.bstartup.com

Join a society, group or club

Signing up to an enterprise society, a local business club or network is good for business (and your social life). Check out these national business and society networks to find your natural fit:

- Enterprise Nation – a friendly community of business owners who benefit from daily content with members receiving profile, free eBooks and member meet-ups plus access to free PR and marketing consultations and a voice to government. www.enterprisenation.com

- 4Networking – national network of business breakfast groups. www.4networking.biz

- NACUE – the national organisation that supports and represents student-led enterprise societies and young entrepreneurs in universities and colleges across the UK. www.nacue.com

- The Gazelle Group – 20-plus further education colleges focused on developing entrepreneurial students and environments. www.thegazellegroup.com

- School for Startups – headed by serial entrepreneur Doug Richard, School for Startups travels the UK hosting events for anyone considering starting a business. www.schoolforstartups.co.uk

- Young Entrepreneur Society – founded by young entrepreneur Carly Ward, this is a network that offers education and monthly events to budding business owners. www.youngentrepreneursociety.org.uk

- Professional Contractors Group (PCG) – if contracting is the life for you, check out the free resources and events hosted by PCG. www.pcg.org.uk

- Virgin Media Pioneers – create a profile and connect with others, plus have the opportunity to pitch to Sir Richard Branson himself via this vibrant network of young entrepreneurs. www.virginmediapioneers.com

As your business grows, why not offer to go and speak to those younger than you who dream of following in your footsteps? Do so by linking up with:

- Peter Jones Enterprise Academy – started by *Dragons' Den* entrepreneur Peter Jones, the academy offers a full-time educational course and qualification in enterprise and entrepreneurship for 16–19 year olds. www.pjea.org.uk

- Young Enterprise – a charity that helps 250,000 young people every year to learn more about business. www.young-enterprise.org.uk

- School Speakers – started by entrepreneur and *Apprentice* TV star Claire Young, this organisation matches enterprising and inspiring speakers with schools. www.schoolspeakers.co.uk

- Inspiring the Future – deliver an enterprising talk at a local school and pass on lessons learned. www.inspiringthefuture.org

Attend trade shows

Promote your brand by attending the shows your customers attend. Research the best shows by reading industry magazines and visiting online forums where people in your sector are talking.

Trade show tactics

Before the event

Negotiate a good deal – if you're prepared to wait it out, the best deals on stands can be had days before the event is starting. The closer the date, the better the price you'll negotiate as the sales team hurry to get a full house.

Tell people you're going – circulate news that you'll be at the event through online networks (giving your location or stand number) and issue a press release if you're doing something newsworthy at the event, maybe launching a new product, having a guest appearance, running a competition, etc.

Be clear on the offer – determine what you are selling at the show and let this be consistent across show materials; from pop-up stands to flyers. Be creative with the stand to keep costs low. Pop-up banners can be bought for £45 each from companies like Demonprint (**www.demonprint.co.uk**). Consider offering a supply of mouth-watering refreshments and branded accessories like pens, bags and t-shirts which can be ordered from companies like Vistaprint (**www.vistaprint.co.uk**).

- Collect data – find ways to collect attendees' names and details. Offer a prize in exchange for business cards or take details in exchange for a follow-up information pack or offer. Some events also offer the facility to scan the details from the delegates' badges (for a fee).

- Take friends/family – invite a supportive team. If you're busy talking to a potential customer, you'll want others on the stand who can be doing the same. If there's time, get to know the exhibitors around you.

- Be prepared – wear comfortable shoes, bring some spare clothes and pack your lunch; if you're busy there may not be time to spend buying food and drink!

After the event

- Follow-up – within a couple of days of returning from the show, contact the people who expressed interest so that interest can be turned into sales.

- Plan ahead – if the show delivered a good return, contact the organisers and ask to be considered for a speaking slot or higher profile at the next event, and confirm your willingness to be a case study testimonial story in any post-show promotion.

Become an expert

If you have a special set of knowledge or experience, set yourself up as an expert in your field and the media will come knocking on your door. Here are eight ways in which you can promote your expertise.

1. Publish a book

Become a published author on your special topic. Utilise the book as a business development tool, taking copies to events, and offering free and downloadable versions to potential customers. Being an author lends you credibility and gives customers information and insight. Get in touch with publishers and agents via *The Writer's & Artist's Yearbook*, or self-publish:

- Blurb | www.blurb.com
- Lulu | www.lulu.com
- Ubyu | www.ubyubooks.com

2. Present yourself

Put yourself forward to speak at events (consider asking for a fee and/or costs to be covered) or suggest being a satellite speaker, where you are beamed in via video link-up, so saving the effort and expense of travel. Invite customers and prospects and make the presentation openly available via SlideShare or Prezi.

- SlideShare | www.slideshare.net
- Prezi | www.prezi.com

3. Host a webinar

Share your expertise or demonstrate a process by hosting a webinar or visual presentation where a live audience can see you and interact. Achieve this via platforms such as GoToMeeting, GoToWebinar and WebEx, and remember to host it at a time that suits your target audience.

- GoToMeeting | www.gotomeeting.com
- GoToWebinar | www.gotomeeting.com/webinar
- WebEx | www.webex.co.uk

4. Produce a film

Maybe the word 'film' is a little ambitious but why not create your own video content and have a sponsored series of guides (or other content) that can be uploaded to video sharing sites such as YouTube, Vimeo and eHow?

- YouTube | www.youtube.com
- Vimeo | www.vimeo.com
- eHow | www.ehow.co.uk

5. Broadcast a podcast

For customers who like to listen to what you have to say at a time that suits them, upload a podcast with top tips, interviews and your thoughts of the day. Make it available on your site, iTunes and Podcast Alley to be sure of a wide audience. Follow the advice below from podcast producer San Sharma on how to record a podcast on a Skype call.

- Submit a podcast to the iTunes store | www.apple.com/itunes/podcasts
- Podcast Alley | www.podcastalley.com

YOU CAN PRODUCE A PODCAST interview using Skype, Pamela Call Recorder, and a little editing know-how. San Sharma shows how it's done, in five simple steps:

1. "Sign up for a free Skype account (**www.skype.com**) and download the Skype software.

2. "If you're using a Windows machine, download Pamela Call Recorder (**www.pamela.biz**), which lets you record your Skype calls. If you're on a Mac, you can download Call Recorder for Skype (**www.ecamm.com**). Both have free trial versions, but only cost around £13 when that's expired.

3. "Call up your interviewee using Skype. If they're a Skype user, too, that will be a free call but if they're on a fixed or mobile line, you'll need to get some Skype Credit (**bit.ly/epymNm**).

4. "Once you've made a connection and agreed with the interviewee the format of the conversation, hit the record button on your call recorder software and you're off!

5. "Edit using Audacity (**audacity.sourceforge.net**), which is free for Windows and Macs, or with GarageBand (**www.apple.com/garageband**), which comes with most Macs (you can also buy it as part of the iLife package).

"The easiest way to share your recording is by uploading it to AudioBoo (**www.audioboo.com**), which lets people listen to it on the web, embedded on your website or via iTunes or a mobile phone."

6. Deliver training

Whether your skill is in embroidering handmade shoes or developing stylish websites, your knowledge could be shared with others. Rather than seeing this as surrendering intelligence to potential competitors, offer instruction you're comfortable with that will create fans and followers who will learn from you, buy from you and, critically, encourage others to do the same. Check out platforms GoToTraining, WebEx and Blackboard, encourage contacts to sign up and then after the demonstration you have a chance to follow up with a group of new contacts.

- GoToTraining | www.gotomeeting.com/fec/training/online_training
- WebEx WebTraining | www.webex.co.uk
- Blackboard | www.blackboard.com

7. Develop an app

Take your content and make an iPhone app. Turn to browser-based platforms such as Appmakr; "AppMakr can be used by anyone with existing content and fans or customers to reach; bloggers/writers, business owners, website owners . . . ".

You can either set a list price to make sales via the App Store or make it available free of charge.

- AppMakr | www.appmakr.com

8. Form groups

Encourage others to discuss, debate and contribute to your content by forming groups utilising social media platforms such as Facebook, LinkedIn and Ning. Bonding interested people to each other will bond them ever closer to you, the content creator and group host.

- Facebook | www.facebook.com
- LinkedIn | www.linkedin.com
- Ning | www.ning.com

BE EVERYWHERE: Keep in touch with existing customers via a newsletter and reach out to the new by making regular appearances at events, on other people's websites and blogs, in newspapers and magazines, and on radio and TV. Write to the magazines and radio stations that ask people to send in their story. It's a free way to get coverage. The more you're covered, the more you'll be invited to speak and comment, and before you know it, you'll be everywhere!

Price point

These options will raise your profile but you can also generate revenue from them. Your options are:

- make your content and knowledge available at no charge to customers, to build your reputation as the go-to person and place for a particular product or service

- charge for access/downloads/viewing and turn your micropublishing activity into a revenue stream in its own right.

This is something you can assess over time. Start with a mix of charged-for and free content, ensure you're providing good value and incentives for your community to remain interested and engaged, and the options to introduce charged-for content will increase.

Embrace social media

Thanks to social media, there have never been so many tools to promote our businesses free of charge. According to research company Nielsen, the world now spends over 110 billion minutes on social networks and blogs per month. That's 22% of all time online, or one in every four and a half minutes. Embrace this and your business will become known. Here are the key tools to use and, crucially, how best to use them.

Facebook

Facebook has over 1 billion users worldwide, so if you need to be where your customers are, there's a good chance some of them will be there!

You can list on Facebook for free and/or advertise on the site and select target audience based on location, sex, age and interests. As an advertiser, you control how much you want to spend and set a daily budget. The minimum budget is US $1.00 (63p) a day. After designing your ad(s), decide for how long you want the campaign to run and whether you want to be charged for the number of clicks you receive (CPC – charge per click) or the number of times your ad is displayed. Visit **www.facebook.com**, create an account, invite friends and contacts to join your group and get promoting.

Download the free eBook *Boost your Business on Facebook* from the Enterprise Nation bookshop: **www.enterprisenation.com/books**.

- **Cost**: free (ads are charged-for)

Twitter

Visit **www.twitter.com**, create an account, follow friends and contacts (and their followers) and get tweeting.

- **Cost**: free

HOW TO BE A SUCCESS ON TWITTER

Twitter expert Mark Shaw (**@markshaw**) shares his four top tips that will have you tweeting like a pro:

1. **"BE COMMITTED.** Add a good photo, perhaps a bespoke background, your URL and an interesting bio. Try and differentiate yourself and make sure the bio contains keywords so that others can find you.

2. **"BE CONSISTENT.** Show up each day and tweet, even if time is short. It's more important to do a small amount each day than lots one day and then nothing for a week or so.

3. **"BE INTERESTING.** Try and tweet three types of messages: social chit-chat; the sharing of resources, links, tools, info, ideas and opinions; and tweets that answer questions which demonstrate your knowledge. Aim for a good balance.

4. **"BE INTERESTED.** Engage with others by answering questions and joining in. Find conversations to enter into via **search.twitter.com** and retweet (RT) other people's messages if they are of interest to you and your followers. It's not about selling things but it is all about building your brand and credibility."

Flickr

Join **www.flickr.com** and promote yourself visually by uploading photos of you and your products or service, and maybe even a few shots of happy customers. The site also carries video clips so you can show:

- events you host, speak at, or attend
- products you make (the finished product) as well as images of the production process
- happy customers wearing/using/enjoying your products and services
- your workspace
- your family (if you – and they – feel comfortable showing your personal side).

You can also easily pull the photos into your blog and social media pages.

- **Cost**: free (option to upgrade to a pro account which is a paid-for package)

LinkedIn

Referring to itself as "the world's largest professional network", LinkedIn has over 100 million members in 200-plus countries. Visit **www.linkedin.com**, create an account and start connecting with contacts and finding new ones. Form LinkedIn groups around your specialist subject.

- **Cost**: free (option to upgrade to a business account, which is a paid-for package)

YouTube

YouTube is the world's most popular online video community, with 24 hours of video uploaded every minute. Start your own business channel for free, and upload videos profiling you and your work.

Create an account (**www.youtube.com/create_account**), start a channel (advice via YouTube video!), and start broadcasting to the world. You can give each of your videos a name and assign keywords to it to help with searching, plus you can have a short description of your company on your profile page. Again, these clips are very easy to add to your website, and they help keep the content fresh and interesting.

- **Cost**: free

Pinterest

Pinterest is a virtual pinboard that lets users organise and share the beautiful things they find on the web. Big brands and small businesses have taken to Pinterest to pin pictures of their products to virtual 'pinboards'. More powerfully, customers are pinning their favourite products – and doing some of the marketing work for them!

The site has just over 2 million daily active users. Head to **tinyurl.com/ENPinterest** to view other Pinteresting facts and figures.

- **Cost:** free

TOTAL BUDGET REQUIRED FOR ONLINE PROMOTION: £0

Measure the results

Time to measure what's working and what's not. Measure media and press mentions through signing up to Google Alerts – and you'll be pleased to know there's a whole host of tools that are free to use and will show real-time results for what's working on your site.

Google Analytics offers intelligence on your website traffic and marketing effectiveness: **www.google.com/analytics**

There are other analytics options:

- Alexa – web traffic metrics, site demographics and top URL listings: **www.alexa.com**

- Clicky – monitors and analyses your site traffic in real time: **www.getclicky.com**

- Opentracker – gather and analyse web stats and monitor online visitors: **www.opentracker.net**

- StatCounter – an invisible web tracker and hit counter that offers data in real time: **www.statcounter.com**

Hopefully what you will see is an upward curve of visitors and time spent on the site.

If you're selling anything, then hopefully this means more sales. If your site is the business, this means you're in a strong position to attract advertisers and begin doing affiliate deals.

MONKEYING AROUND: Run a poll with, for example, Wufoo (**www.wufoo.com**) or Survey Monkey (**www.surveymonkey.com**). Both are free to use, then publish the results via a press release and online. The media loves good polls!

Look out, in particular, for the sources of your traffic (which are your highest referring sites) and your most popular pages. You can see days where your site receives spikes in visitor levels (and track this back to marketing) and measure if visitors are spending longer periods on the site and which times are popular, e.g. weekends, evenings, lunchtimes, etc.

Use the following template to ensure you're making the most of all your marketing opportunities.

Template 7: Marketing and Promotion

Media

Press (local and national)
List relevant names and journalists

Radio
List programmes on which you'd like to appear

Television
List programmes on which you'd like to appear

Magazines
List target titles

Online
List target sites

Other

Events
List events to attend; networking and trade. What about hosting your own event, too?

Awards

List awards relevant to your business and their dates of entry

Your social network

Plan of action for engaging with major social networks on ongoing basis

III. GROW

With marketing and sales underway, you are getting known and making money. Now it's time to grow your profits by outsourcing, keeping the business in balance, staying on top of cash flow and getting some good support.

66 Write your own rules –
whilst you shouldn't
ignore advice from other
successful entrepreneurs,
don't be a slave to their
methods. You know your
business best and can
navigate your own way. **99**

– Jess Butcher,
founder, Blippar

13. ATTRACT CUSTOMERS BACK

You are making sales via your site and developing a strong community of fans and followers. Give visitors and customers a reason to return with content that is regularly updated.

If you have a blog, try to post regularly, and if you're selling, keep the product range updated. Give your site some TLC each day, as fresh content will attract visitors who want to see what's new and will also appeal to the trawling web spiders who determine search engine results.

User-generated content

Encourage your site visitors to get to know each other through a forum or comment boxes. Before you know it, a sense of community will develop and visitors will log on each day to find out who's saying what and what's happening with whom.

Exclusive offers

Extend offers to your existing customers, readers or members that will tempt them back. This offer could be conditional on customers referring a friend: that way your customer returns to the site with others in tow. Add to this with a badge of honour; design an icon that visitors can display on their own site to show their affiliation with you.

Guest appearances

Invite special guests to appear on your site via guest blog posts, hosting a webchat or a featured interview.

Keep in touch

Communicate all these good and sticky things to your users through a regular e-newsletter powered by sites such as MailChimp (**www.mailchimp.com**), Constant Contact (**www.constantcontact.com**) or AWeber Communications (**www.aweber.com**).

Email marketing: keep it clean, keep it simple, keep it relevant

Email marketing works best when it is targeted. This means keeping your lists clean and organising them according to previous customer contact. A well-segmented list means you can send more frequent campaigns, ensuring a steady flow of business, without worrying about clogging up inboxes. Keep your email designs clean and simple – making it easier for your customer to make informed buying decisions in a snap.

14. FOCUS ON WHAT YOU DO BEST AND OUTSOURCE THE REST

The business is growing, time is your most precious resource and you are in need of help. The quickest and most affordable place to get it is from other companies with whom you can partner to get projects done, as well as from expert advisors and mentors who will offer advice on how the business can continue to grow.

With outsourcing you can free yourself up to dedicate your attention to sales, strategy or whatever the business activity is that you do best. My advice to all businesses is always: *focus on what you do best and outsource the rest*.

What can be outsourced and to whom?

Admin

Hire a VA (virtual assistant) to do the admin tasks you don't want or don't have the time to do. Find skilled VAs via sites such as

- Worldwide101 | worldwide101.com

and

- Time Etc | www.timeetc.com

Accounts

Unless you are in the accountancy business, this is almost a must to be outsourced. Monthly payroll, accounts, VAT returns and corporate tax returns all take time and it's time you can't afford or simply don't have. A cost/benefit analysis is likely to show that it's cheaper to outsource to a qualified accountant. Ask around for recommendations of accountants in your area who deliver a quality service at a competitive cost and are registered with the Institute of Chartered Accountants for England and Wales (ICAEW). As mentioned earlier, you can benefit from up to three free consultations with ICAEW accountants via the Business Advice Service (**www.businessadviceservice.com**).

For online accounting and invoicing that makes life easier for you and your accountant, check out:

- FreeAgent | **www.freeagent.com**
- SageOne | **www.sageone.co.uk**
- QuickBooks | **www.quickbooks.co.uk**

PR, marketing and design

Outsource your PR to a specialist who can be pitching and promoting the business whilst you're at work. Find skilled professionals on directory sites such as Enterprise Nation (**www.enterprisenation.com**), oDesk (**www.odesk.com**) and PeoplePerHour (**www.peopleperhour.com**) and make the most of a free PR consultation with Enterprise Nation's head of media, Liz Slee.

Sales

Hire a sales expert to make calls, set up appointments and attend trade shows. Find these professionals online, contact telemarketing companies that offer outbound sales calls as a service, or look at sales specialists such as Winning Sales (**www.winningsales.co.uk**).

Customer service

Looking after customers is vital, but even that can be outsourced. Get Satisfaction's tagline is "people-powered customer service" – it provides a web-hosted platform, much like a forum, where customers can ask questions, suggest improvements, report a problem or give praise. This and other online customer satisfaction tools can save you time and money by having the power of the crowd take care of customer questions!

- Get Satisfaction | www.getsatisfaction.com
- Zen Desk | www.zendesk.com

IT

Spending too many hours trying to fix a single IT problem? Outsource the hassle and save your time, money and blood pressure. Find IT professionals online or contact IT support teams connected to the large retailers.

- Geeks-on-Wheels | www.geeks-on-wheels.com
- Knowhow | www.knowhow.com
- Geek Squad | www.geeksquad.co.uk

Steps to successful outsourcing

Do the groundwork

Spend some time working on the task yourself so you've built foundations before handing it over to someone else. For example, if you outsource sales then have a ready-made contacts list and some open doors that the specialist can build on, rather than starting from scratch. This will make it more cost-effective for you and means that they hit the ground running.

Be clear on the brief

Having spent some time doing the task yourself, you will have a clear idea of the brief. Back to the example of outsourcing sales, if you've spent 6–12 months sourcing leads and making contacts, you'll have a much clearer idea of the type of work the specialist should do.

The clearer the brief, the better the results.

Take your time

And take references. Spend time evaluating the specialists in the market and, if you can, talk to their existing clients. Do they have the industry experience you're after? Will they represent your brand in a professional manner? Have they delivered a good job for other clients? When an outsourced arrangement works well, the partner becomes part of your team – so choose them as carefully as you would choose an employee.

Let go!

Outsourcing means having to let go a little. Someone else becomes accountable for these results. Embrace this rather than resist it. As the business owner you remain in ultimate control but the expert will need their own space in which to flourish. Outsourcing can save you time and help make you money. Finding the right partner, on the right terms, will make you feel like a new and liberated person.

Form teams

Once you've chosen your outsourced partner(s), it's important to keep in regular contact and work together as a team. There are a number of online project management and collaboration tools to help you stay on top of projects and in control of the company.

- Basecamp (**www.basecamp.com**) is the project management tool we rely on at Enterprise Nation. This is a top-class product that allows you to create projects, invite people to view them, upload files and make comments. It's effective online project management that can be accessed from anywhere.

- Share documents via Google Docs (**docs.google.com**). You can edit on the move, choose who accesses documents and share changes in real time.

- Huddle (**www.huddle.com**) offers simple and secure online workspaces. Huddle is hosted, so there's no software to download and it's free to get started.

Solutions to enable group-talk

- GoToMeeting | **www.gotomeeting.com**
Work with anyone, anywhere with this easy to use online meeting tool.

- Ketchup | **www.useketchup.com**
Share and record meeting notes.

- Powwownow | www.powwownow.co.uk

Free conference calling at 'open access' level. Priced packages available.

- OmniJoin | webconferencing.brother.co.uk

Hold secure and reliable meetings in high definition video and high quality VoIP (Voice over IP) audio with up to 50 people.

Form partnerships

If relationships develop, you may decide to form a partnership. Consider writing a partnership agreement as your pre-nup in business. At the outset of a relationship, all is good and you're excited about the potential, but it's best to be safe; have the terms written and agreed so that all parties are clear on expectations.

The following should not be taken as concrete legal advice, more of a guideline on how to draw up an agreement.

Scope of agreement

What is your partnership working to achieve? For example, "This agreement is made between Company A and Company B. The agreement is related to the generation of online advertising revenues/hosting of an event/development of a new product."

Respective responsibilities

Set out the expectations on who does what. For example, Company A will be responsible for promotion and business development and Company B will take on technical development and client care. Also include a note of how you'll keep each other briefed, maybe through the use of an online project management tool.

Finances

What will be the split in revenue, and is this before or after costs? And who owns the intellectual property of the product/service/activity? Consider including a clause that states the agreement will be reviewed in six months so that both parties can check on progress and have the right to cease the agreement if it hasn't gone as planned.

Be fair

Agreements where both parties feel that they're receiving their fair share are likely to be longer-lasting than those when one party feels embittered. Talk about this before writing and concluding the agreement. Make sure there's no resentment or sense of being exploited on either side.

Sign it!

After making the effort to produce an agreement, be sure to sign it! And then store it so that you can access it easily if the need arises.

When writing the clauses in your agreement, think about all the things that could go wrong and safeguard against them. It's a practical exercise and won't harm your newly formed business relationship but will get it off on a firm footing. If you're looking for a template agreement, check out sites such as **www.clickdocs.co.uk**.

BUSINESS OWNER PLUS ONE: When the business is at a stage to take on its first new employee, visit the 'Growing your business' section of the GOV.UK site (**www.gov.uk/growing-your-business/hire-and-train-staff**), which offers details on how to employ and your obligations as an employer over time.

15. KEEP THE BUSINESS IN BALANCE

As the business continues to grow, you will want to maintain momentum and grow at a comfortable pace. Achieve this by following what I call 'the golden triangle', which will keep you and the business in balance. This requires spending roughly a third of your time on three key things:

1. Customer care

Look after your customers by delivering a quality product or service, on time and within budget. And remember . . . the customer is always right!

I ask clients for feedback so that I can keep a check on what they're thinking and changes they'd like to see. It's good to know some personal details about your customers, too. (Maybe their birthday, their favourite hobby.) As you gather these details, make a quick note so you can send a birthday card on the right date, etc. Don't go overboard, but showing that you care certainly won't harm your relationship.

Offer customers good service, regular communication and an innovative line of products and services. It will stand you in good stead.

2. New business

Taking care of customers means taking care of sales. Why? Because it costs less to win business from existing customers than it does to find new ones. If customers are happy, they'll say good things about you to new and potential customers. This is called word-of-mouth marketing and achieving it is every business owner's dream!

Secure new clients through marketing, encouraging recommendations, and direct-sales calls and pitches.

3. Admin

Not as enjoyable as the first two, but it still has to be done. Keep the books in order by raising invoices in good time, being on top of cash flow, and filing tax returns and company documents on time and in order. In short, keep the finances in check and the books up-to-date.

Cash is king

In Chapter 9 we looked at the topic of straightforward finance and how to plan income and outgoings.

Keep an eye on the accounts so you can see how much money is in the bank, how much is owed and whether this covers your outgoings.

This is a vital part of running your business and something you will need to keep close tabs on especially at the start. Monitor this using your accounts software and online banking. It's a very well-worn phrase in business, but cash is most definitely king.

Getting paid and paying others

A key part in managing your cash flow is making sure you get paid and get paid promptly. How you get paid will depend quite a lot on the type of business you have and whether you are selling direct to customers or to other businesses. If selling directly, you will mostly be paid immediately. If you are dealing with other businesses, the chances are most will expect to pay on invoice (more on this below) and will expect a credit period in which to pay. Be prepared to offer credit terms, but be careful about how long you give, how much credit you'll allow and who you offer this to.

If you need to buy in products or services from others as part of your business it's always worth seeing if you too can arrange credit terms with suppliers. This should help you balance payments in and out. This isn't always easy at the start and you may have to pay upfront to begin with, but it is something to ask for. Having built up a good relationship with your supplier it should be a natural next step.

Invoices

Be on time with invoicing and keep a record of amounts outstanding. I have a simple spreadsheet with five columns labelled 'client', 'invoice amount', 'invoice number', 'date submitted' and 'date paid'.

- Your invoices should be a simple document with basic details. The less cause for question on the invoice, the faster it will be paid.

- Always find out in advance who should be named on the invoice, where it should be sent and whether you need to include any sort of order reference number. When dealing with large companies in particular, this sort of thing can make a big difference to how quickly you get paid.

- Settle invoices as promptly as you can. Your suppliers should be grateful and repay you with good service.

See the next page for an example invoice.

Hopefully your clients and customers will always pay promptly, but occasionally you might need to remind them. Do this politely and clearly. It's often sensible to send a monthly statement to a client detailing any outstanding invoices, and usually that's enough to spur them into action.

You can balance the budget with a piece of accounting software. See 'Accounts' earlier for details of options, and don't forget to have a look at the offers available in this kit.

Receipts

Keep business-related receipts in a place where they're easy to find. I have a big wicker box that I use as a collecting place for receipts. It's helpful that they're all in one place when it's time to do the VAT return.

Track your time with time-tracking software

- Cashboard | www.getcashboard.com

- Four Four Time | www.fourfourtime.co.uk

- TraxTime | www.spudcity.com/traxtime

SAMPLE INVOICE

1. Name of your contact

2. The date

3. An address to which the cheque shall be sent or bank details for accounts in which monies should be deposited

4. Company registration and VAT number (if applicable)

5. Invoice number and client's purchase order (PO) number

6. Payment terms (e.g. payable within 30 days of receipt), and by cheque, transfer, etc.

7. A brief product description or summary of services

8. Amount owing (inclusive or exclusive of VAT, depending on whether you're registered).

I think it's good practice to include a cover note, too, that confirms what's being invoiced and thanks the client for their custom.

Invoice

YOUR SMALL BUSINESS

1.
Attention: Joe Smith
Managing Director
A. N. Other Small Business
321 First Street
Anytown, County AB1 2CD
Date 29/01/2012 **2.**

3.
Your small business address
123 Second Street
Anothertown, County AB2 3CD
T 01234 567 8910
F 01234 567 8911
you@youremailaddress.com
http://www.yourwebsite.com/

4.
Your company registration
VAT no. 12345678910

PROJECT TITLE: A. N. Other Small Business website
PROJECT DESCRIPTION: Redesign of business website **5.**
INVOICE NUMBER: 01
TERMS: 30 days **6.**

7.

8.

Description	Amount owed
Graphic design	£1,500.00
Programming	£2,000.00
Hosting	£500.00
Total	**£4,000.00**

Please make cheque payable to Your Name and deliver to the address printed on this invoice.

Sincerely yours,

Your Name

16. SUPPORT

All of the success stories in this kit have spoken of the valuable support received from friends, family, advisors and experienced entrepreneurs.

Ask questions at every opportunity and build a support network. Here's where to look for people who are happy to help.

Peers

Who better to turn to than those going through the same experience as you? Visit the sites below and join their active communities of business owners.

- Enterprise Nation | www.enterprisenation.com
- Business Zone | www.businesszone.co.uk
- Start Up Donut | www.startupdonut.co.uk
- Smarta | www.smarta.com
- Startups | startups.co.uk
- Fresh Business Thinking | www.freshbusinessthinking.com
- School for Startups | www.schoolforstartups.co.uk

Mentors

Find a mentor through making a direct approach to experts, professionals and business owners you admire and respect. Or source one via government website Mentorsme.co.uk.

And don't restrict yourself to one mentor! I have learnt from many people as my businesses have passed through different stages of development. My approach was to get in touch with the person I felt best placed to have the answer, take on board their views, consider my options, and then act.

In my view, the ideal mentor is someone who possesses four things:

1. experience of your industry/sector

2. the ability to listen

3. the technical skills to advise

4. a willingness to make introductions to useful contacts.

If you can find these in one person, you are very fortunate indeed.

One of the finest things a mentor can do is allow you to talk. By doing so, you often work out the answer. Sometimes you just need an experienced sounding board.

Business advisors

Find experts and business advisors on the Enterprise Nation marketplace. The marketplace is filled with talented professionals who can help with everything from sales and marketing to leadership and management, and how to make the most of digital technologies. Search for an expert by location or sector specialism and surround yourself with top talent from the start.

- Enterprise Nation Marketplace | **www.enterprisenation.com/marketplace**

Accelerate!

And finally . . . if you want to give your business an extra injection and growth spurt, check out some of the 'Accelerators' launched by companies to give you space, funding and access to mentors, technology and customers.

- Wayra | wayra.org/en
- School for Creative Startups | www.schoolforcreativestartups.com
- Accelerator Academy | www.acceleratoracademy.com
- The Bakery | www.thebakerylondon.com
- Collider 13 | collider13.com/about
- New Entrepreneurs Foundation | www.newentrepreneursfoundation.co.uk
- Entrepreneur First | www.entrepreneurfirst.org.uk
- TechStars | www.techstars.com/program/locations/london
- Microsoft BizSpark | www.microsoft.com/BizSpark
- GrowthAccelerator | www.growthaccelerator.com
- Level 39 | www.level39.co

THE BEST OF LUCK

You've read the stories, devoured the tips and completed the templates. It's time to take your own idea, passion, hobby or skill, and turn it into a business.

I hope what you've picked up from this kit is that regardless of your age, background or sector, if you're starting out as your own boss there's support all around. In whichever direction you turn, you'll find people to cheer you along and answer your questions; you'll find loans on offer and resources on tap.

Make the most of this support and never be afraid to seek help or approach mentors. With guidance from those who've trodden the entrepreneurial path, you will find your own way and build a future that offers financial reward and freedom in your working life.

Start-ups are most definitely the new rock stars and I see no sign of this wearing out any time soon. Big companies want to be seen alongside you and customers want to buy from you. These are good conditions in which to start a new venture.

So, now it's over to you. And even though this farewell is entitled 'Best of Luck', one of my favourite quotes is one that's well known and came from golf pro Gary Player, who said: "The harder I practise, the luckier I get."

My advice to you: go practise and get lucky!

EMMA JONES | @EMMALJONES

HOW ENTERPRISE NATION CAN HELP

Enterprise Nation helps thousands of people in the UK turn their good ideas into great businesses.

There's lots of free advice on our website and events, where you can get together with other start-ups and would-be entrepreneurs to learn from experience and from experts. You'll find essential business books too.

And when you join Enterprise Nation, you get 25% off everything, as well as free meet-ups and exclusive benefits.

Find out more at **www.enterprisenation.com** – and don't forget to save over £500 on essentials for your new business at **www.enterprisenation.com/offers**

WITH THANKS

To the following people who have contributed their expertise, story or tip in the compilation of this kit:

The start-ups

Jordan Bourke | **Guilt Free Gourmet**

Philip Crilly | **Eatibles**

David Galbraith | **SWIG Flasks**

Paula Hutchings | **Marketing Vision Consultancy**

Sally Guyer | **Cambridge Raincoat Company**

Sinead Koehler | **Crafty Fox Market**

Carol Lovell | **Stowe London**

Eleanor Stuart | **Eleanor Stuart**

Dean Tempest | **Linkee**

Esther Thompson | **Tea Huggers**

Alexandra Van Berckel | **Pinucci**

Tilly Walnes | **Tilly And The Buttons**

Experts

Emily Coltman | **FreeAgent**

Tamsin Fox-Davies | **Constant Contact**

Katie McPhee | **Eventbrite**

Laura Rigney | **Pitcher House**

Mark Shaw | **Twitter expert**

Greg Simpson | **Press For Attention**

Jackie Wade | **Winning Sales**

Dan Wilson | **Tamebay**

Joanna Tall | **Off To See My Lawyer**

Andy Yates | **Angel investor**

Enterprise Nation

San Sharma

Myles Hunt

Lorna Bladen

Liz Slee

Chris Read

Chris Parker